Résumés for The Smart Job Search

The Ultimate Guide to Writing Résumés in the 90s

Read Résumés for The Smart Job Search and get the job you deserve!

ABOUT THE AUTHOR

Marc L. Makos is president of Smart Résumés in Boston, Massachusetts. His company puts together the packages clients need to successfully compete for the best jobs. Mr. Makos looks forward to any correspondence you may be inclined to write. He may be reached as follows:

Marc L. Makos
c/o HD Publishing
P.O. Box 2171
Boston, MA 02106

Mr. Makos is also the author of The Smart Job Search—A Guide to Proven Methods for Finding a Great Job, published by HD Publishing in November, 1991. In this book, Mr. Makos offers 308 pages and 21 chapters covering all aspects of the job search. Readers learn how best to handle research, answer job ads, interview (with over 100 questions explained and sample answers given for each), write their résumés and cover letters, follow-up on leads and prospects, and more.

Mr. Makos is also preparing separate books on interviewing and writing cover letters, both to be released in 1994.

▼

Résumés for The Smart Job Search

The Ultimate Guide to Writing Résumés in the 90s

Marc L. Makos

HD Publishing
▸ Boston, Massachusetts ◂

▸ *Résumés for The Smart Job Search:*
The Ultimate Guide to Writing Résumés in the '90s

Copyright © 1993 by Marc L. Makos

▸ *Library of Congress Cataloging–in–Publication Data*

Makos, Marc L., 1960 -
    Résumés for the smart job search : the ultimate guide to writing
résumés in the 90s / Marc L. Makos. — 1st ed.

            p.   cm.
    Includes index.
    ISBN 0-9630394-9-0 : $14.95
    1. Résumés (Employment) 2. Job hunting—United States.
    3. Employment agencies—United States—Directories. I. Title.
    HF5383.M236 1993
    808'.06665—dc20

                                                    92-47008
                                                        CIP

▸ *Cover Design and Desktop Publishing Production by*
Carlos Chiyoda, Boston, MA

1st Edition
Printed in the United States of America

Published by:
HD Publishing
Post Office Box 2171
Boston, MA 02106 U.S.A.

HD Publishing books are available at special discounts for bulk purchases for public and private groups, employment agencies, premium, fund raising, or educational use. Special editions or book excerpts can also be created to specification.

For details contact:
Special Purchases
HD Publishing
Post Office Box 2171
Boston, MA 02106 U.S.A.

▸ *Warning - Disclaimer*

This book provides valuable advice regarding the subject matter at hand. Still, this book is sold with the understanding that the publisher and author are not providing any legal or accounting services, nor any guarantee that your adherence to methods presented herein will produce any failures or successes.

This book cannot publish every known piece of material that exists on writing a résumé, but attempts to be a leading resource in the field and complement other texts. You should read as much material as possible.

Every individual must expect to invest much time and effort in their job search. Every possible consideration has been made to make this book accurate and timely to the current job market. Still, mistakes, both typographical and in content, might be found.

Therefore, this book should be used as one of your guides to preparing for career and life choices. No book should be used as the only, "ultimate" source of information. The more you know, the better. The more you read, the more you'll learn and profit in the future. We think this book educates as well as provides timely information.

The author and publisher have neither responsibility nor liability to any person, group or entity with respect to any and all losses or damages caused, that may be alleged to be caused, directly or in any indirect way by the information presented in this book.

The author and publisher have made their best efforts in preparing this book. These efforts include the research and testing of the material to determine their viability. Still, the author and publisher make no warranty of any kind, expressed or implied, regarding the suggestions and instructions contained in this book. Further, the author and publisher make no warranties of any kind regarding the services of any public or private agencies, institutions, etc. which are listed in this book.

The author and publisher shall not be liable in the event of any or all incidental or consequential damages connected to, or arising from, the furnishing, performance or use of the instructions, and/or claims of productivity or monetary gains or losses.

If you do not wish to be bound by any and all conditions listed above, you should return this book for a refund to your point of purchase. To do so, return the book and all original materials received with purchase. Books should be returned as received. Remember, no refunds will be given for used, damaged material or books which have been written in.

▸ *Trademarks*

Trademarked names appear in various parts of this book, particularly in the chapter of résumé examples. Instead of listing the names and entities that own these trademarks or insert a trademark symbol every time the trademarked name is mentioned, the publisher and author state that the trademarked names are used only for editorial purposes and to the benefit of the trademark owner with absolutely no intention of infringing upon that trademark.

▸ *Table of Contents*

INTRODUCTION

In our offices in Boston, Massachusetts, a client wanted help writing his résumé. Part of the conversation went like this:

"What field do you want to move into?"
"Television."
"Do you have experience related to that field."
"Yes. I've had my current job for 3 years, but before that I worked as a research assistant for a company dealing with the entertainment industries. It lasted for 3 years."
"Great! Let's focus on that experience when we write your résumé."
"I can't do that! I just got promoted to head waiter. I'm a great worker. They'll want to know about that!"

Maybe they will. Maybe not. Probably not as the first piece of information on the résumé.

No matter how great you are at what you do, employers want to know how you'll benefit THEM. We're taught the past is the past, the present is what we make it, and the future awaits. While true, you must consider how your past and present work history will benefit your future employer. Remember this—employers want to know how your PAST will benefit THEIR future.

An employer wants to know if you have the years and/or level of experience for the job. The employer wants to know if you will be a contributor, a team player, a leader, a person who will accomplish more and more and help the company prosper. Further, the employer wants to look at your résumé and think that you are a better, more qualified candidate than the competition — the other résumés stacked high on their desk!

Our example about the waiter shows what can happen when a person cannot gain distance from personal emotions when writing their résumé. Throughout the rest of this book, you must look impartially and objectively at your work and life history.

► *Quick Tip*

Because the résumé is considered by many the 2nd most important document you'll ever create (the first being your will), take a lawyer's approach to its creation. And at first, pretend you're writing someone else's résumé.

Gather all facts. Analyze how those facts benefit your client (you), then write short statements describing why this information is important to the case. Then, rewrite the information so the audience sides with you when giving their verdict (to employ or not to employ…).

How Many Versions of My Résumé?

To know what to write on your résumé you have to know what a company wants and needs from an ideal employee for the position. Does this mean you'll need a different résumé for every company? Absolutely not. It simply means that you cannot get caught up in technical terms—"lingoisms" which might confuse an employer and put you out of the running. The woman selling cars and the man selling mutual funds are not equally experienced in sales. Each has their own market. Know your industry or field. Know what basic skills are needed. Translate the wording of your abilities according to their needs.

▸ *The Résumé Examples*

We have found that as much as we write about each part of the résumé, the examples are what people identify with most easily and ask for in more depth. Therefore, while each part of the résumé will be fully explained, each chapter will show many examples to help you when writing your own résumé.

Various suggestions and details are explained regarding the sample résumé, including layout decisions, typefaces, category choices, etc. You may be able to identify with an example, then agree or disagree with the various suggestions made. Whatever you think about each résumé, you will be able to make better and stronger decisions about your own material and presentation.

▸ *"Before" and "After"*

Now a word of caution. No typewriter, computer or piece of advanced technology guarantees a great résumé. My company, Smart Résumés, in Boston, has been creating thousands of résumés over the years. Content, layout, design, typeface, font, paper stock, stylization—whether using bold, underlined, or italicized lettering, etc., and many other considerations determine whether your résumé is a success.

We believe that the typewriter is really an outmoded instrument for producing a great résumé. We are strong advocates of Macintosh computers and Postscript laser printers. In fact, we will only use Macintosh computers at our company. We believe these machines have revolutionized great parts of our society. We also believe that Postscript laser printers enable every company and individual to elegantly represent themselves and their products.

▸ *What to Look Out For*

There are some very general guidelines for you to follow when writing and presenting your résumé. The following are some of the most important things to be aware of:

1. Length. Preferably, your résumé should by one page in length. I suggest if you offer over 10 years of professional experience, you may expand the résumé to two pages. Even so, do know that I have written many résumés for people making well over $50,000 yearly who do very nicely with a one page résumé.

In academia, I do recognize that a résumé often becomes the "curriculum vitae" and demands a listing of graduate, undergraduate, and other studies, lists of all presentations one has participated in and publications one has written for, and a host of other necessary categories and pieces of information. The general résumé writer does not have the same concerns as the academic (professor, scientist, etc.) and should not be subject to the grandiose thought that their material is important enough to go on for as many pages as desired.

2. Easy to Read. This does not mean you must use the most basic language to deliver your mes-

sage. But you should be able to present your message so that the employer can easily find the material of interest to them. If you have had five different jobs and you capitalize the name of your first company on the résumé, logically you should capitalize all of the companies remaining. Similarly, if you put a job title under the company name, for example, all job titles should be listed under the other company names.

3. Poor Categorization. As you'll read later in the book, there are many categories you may choose to list on your résumé. Of course you will not go overboard and list 12 or 15 categories. The reader of your document must want to read the material. You have to make sure where you put things on the page makes sense. For example, I would sub-categorize "Honors: Dean's List" under "EDUCATION" instead of giving it its own category somewhere else on the page. Make the reading process logical for the reader.

4. White Space. I tell my customers not to write their résumé so that the reader must get a cup of coffee, pull up a chair, settle into the cushion, and get ready to wade through ALL THAT TEXT — you'll never get the thing read! Instead, say what you have to say but leave enough white space on the page so that reading the document is enlightening and exciting. If the employer can read your résumé while running down the hallway to an important meeting starting in two minutes — and be impressed with your presentation — you have succeeded.

5. Design. You must arrive at a nice balance in your presentation. Your left and right margins should be the same size. The top and bottom of your document should be visually pleasing. A tip I suggest to you is to allow no more than 3/4" from the top of the page to where your name is on the page. Anything more and the document has a look as if it has somehow "slipped" down the page. Also, if the bottom of the page has too much space, adjust the space between your categories to stretch the length of your résumé to one full page.

6. Errors. It's a brutal world and if you have misspellings — "typos" — on the page, you have severely hurt your chances. A professional service should offer spell checking, but don't fool yourself into thinking a "spell checker" guarantees no mistakes. A spell checker won't catch a "the the" on the page, nor will it find that "organized wars for the home show" should have been "organized wares for the home show." Check your résumé thoroughly. At Smart Résumés, I am very concerned that we give a perfect document to our client. Still, we show everyone a proof that they must check and approve for printing. If necessary, redoing or reprinting your résumé is much better than never getting an interview. Ultimately, it's a lot less costly, too.

Do read through all the chapters and make notes along the way before attempting to write out your résumé in detail. Hopefully, this book will offer many valuable insights into producing a great résumé. The résumé you create may affect tens or hundreds of thousands of dollars in future income, or income potential. (Think of a $25,000 job held for 6 years. That's $150,000!) Take the time to do the best you can possibly do.

▶ *For Our Mail-Order Clients*

I know you will take great care in producing your résumé. Should you decide my company's services would be helpful, we offer competitive prices for producing great résumés for clients throughout the United States and delivering them through the mail in a timely manner.

Please refer to the "Conclusion" chapter of the book for a listing on how to use our services.

JOB OBJECTIVE

▼
AKA's:

Career Objective	*Job Objective*	*Objective*
Summary	*Career Goal*	*Qualified By*

If used, the job objective may be the most important part of your résumé for a very simple reason. All your years of experience, the extra classes you took to improve skills, your education, and more will not have any importance if the employer doesn't get to it on the page. If the job objective isn't successful, the résumé fails. The objective of the job objective is to get the reader to read on.

How do you make that happen?

First, know what the companies in your field want in a valued employee. Second, understand how what you've done in the past would benefit the employer in the future. And third, translate those skills into one power statement that makes the reader want to know more about you. It's that simple. And that difficult.

▶ *Note*

We frequently write résumés for clients without any job objective. This is acceptable depending on what your total job search methods are going to be. For example, if you are responding to job advertisements or other leads and plan to write cover letters for each, a job objective is not a necessity. The cover letter will act as the "lead in" and should entice the reader enough to read the résumé. Of course, be prepared to write a great cover letter!

Also, in-person responses may allow you to do without a job objective. Walking into an office with a "Hello, my name is Sarah Jones and I'm interested in applying for the position of Finish Carpenter for the Stanhope project" may eliminate the need to write the job objective.

The job objective should be written in such a way as to eliminate the possibility for the employer to think you are not qualified or that you wouldn't make the right "fit" for the position. If you write "To be a sous chef" and the employer desperately needs an all-around assistant to the master chef, with part-time responsibility for table presentations and Thursday nights as fill-in "jack of all trades", you may have hurt your chances for getting the job. On the other hand, should you write "To use 7 years of proven restaurant experience where knowledge of all aspects of kitchen operations in a fine dining setting will be fully utilized" your chances will probably increase significantly.

The trick is to present yourself, in one statement, as a competent, well-rounded, and multi-talented individual. Let's look at a number of examples so that you can see how the job objective may open up more great opportunities. As you read the examples, think of all you've done and how you might write a job objective to entice the employer.

Accountant

To build on a strong academic record in accounting and business administration to eventually become certified as a public accountant.

Accountant

A challenging, growth-oriented position with an organization where expertise in accounting and corporate financial management will be fully utilized.

Administrative Assistant

Offering proven office support skills in professional environments. Supporting staff and team members to achieve departmental goals.

Administrator

To contribute strong professional and academic experience to a position with increasing responsibilities in a growth oriented organization.

Customer Service

Utilizing proven experience in sales and customer relations to obtain a position with a progressive organization.

Division Executive

Utilizing proven professional experience as a Division Executive to contribute to the training programs of a leading, growth-oriented organization.

Drafter

Utilizing solid architectural experience to ensure completion of projects and overall company success.

Entry-Level Position

To work in an entry-level position that will lead to a management training program.

Financial Services Professional

To utilize proven and extensive service skills to tailor products and services according to client and corporate goals in a banking environment.

Generalist

To utilize proven professional experience in order to contribute to a challenging and responsible position for a progressive company.

Generalist

Seeking a position utilizing skills and experience with a progressive organization that offers long term development and growth.

Health Care Professional

To advance the goals of a marketing-driven health care company, where there is opportunity for creative/innovative revenue-building ideas.

Health Care Worker

Seeking a position in a health care or day environment where direct experience will provide immediate benefits to an employer.

Intern

To obtain an intern position in the legal field that would utilize a strong academic background and provide demanding and valuable work experience.

International Marketing

To utilize proven knowledge and experience to pursue a marketing career that rewards performance; U.S. resident with extensive travel throughout U.S. and Europe and knowledge of four languages.

Manager

To utilize over 4 years of proven management skills and a strong academic record to contribute to the long term goals of a leading company.

Manager

Executive management position with bottom line responsibility.

Marketing Representative

Responsible marketing position with a major corporation.

Marketing Representative

Sales and marketing professional with a proven record of success in high value sales.

Music Production

A position in the music business where strong academic and internship experience will contribute to the growth of an innovative label.

Operations Manager

Seeking a career in operational planning and budget analysis, where data processing, reporting, and bookkeeping expertise will be fully utilized.

Physician's Assistant

Seeking position as a physician assistant or participating in the medical field while finishing coursework to complete degree requirements.

Sales Manager

Seeking senior sales management position in the food industry, offering expertise in the areas of merchandising, sales forecasting, marketing, and promotions. Successful track record in managing route salesmen, account executives, and broker networks.

Salesperson

An ambitious, organized, self-motivated individual who seeks employment within a growth-oriented company which offers solid career development based on performance.

Salesperson

To obtain a sales position in a growth company offering career advancement based upon performance.

Salesperson

A challenging, growth-oriented position with 4 years of proven experience in sales and a commitment to achieve corporate goals.

Senior Executive

A senior executive position where over 14 years of proven expertise in business development will contribute to long-term corporate growth.

Systems Analyst

Utilizing proven systems expertise to contribute as a Hardware, System or Technical Support Analyst where customer service is a top priority.

Teacher

To exercise proven academic and teaching expertise in Art History to contribute at the junior college level

Telemarketer

Using interpersonal skills to assist in marketing services and developing products.

Theatre Designer

Since 1982, independent success as an Art Director and Designer. Recognized for innovative and award-winning designs in leading playhouses.

Volunteer

A position where dedicated and responsible work performance, the ability to communicate effectively, and good human relations will contribute to the achievement of an organization's goals.

The job objective should intrigue the reader enough to make her read on. In my other book, The Smart Job Search — A Guide to Proven Methods for Finding a Great Job, I suggested you apply my "we don't need" to your job objective.

If you can write "we don't need" in front a your job objective, you have not written a great job objective. An employer might very well say "we don't need an architect's assistant," but would be much less likely to say "we don't need sold architectural experience to ensure completion of projects within time and budget deadlines." Do you see the difference?

As you should have realized, these job objectives tell the employer what you want but, more importantly, suggest to the employer what you plan to do for THEM! Read through the rest of the chapters to decide whether or not you need a job objective on your résumé.

SUMMARY OF QUALIFICATIONS

▼
AKA's:

Summary of Strengths	*Summarized Qualifications*	*Summary Statement*
Summarized By	*Background*	*Expertise*
Skills	*Profile*	*Career Focus*
Performance Highlights	*Special Skills*	*Primary Experience*
Highlighted Activities	*Professional Qualifications*	*Career Highlights*
Strengths	*Accomplishments*	

Now that you have gotten their attention with the job objective, you may want to present a quick summary of those qualities employers need to succeed in business. I believe a summary of qualifications can be a wonderful way to tell the employer "you need me! Take a quick look at the things I can do!"

The job objective identifies your purpose as related to their needs. The summary of qualifications takes the powerful skills you have and presents them as an enticement to the reader. Strength by strength, your only goal is to have the reader say—"Tell me more! Tell me more!"

The result you are looking for is to get an interview. In the worst of times, most people are employed. If you and your résumé show confidence and conviction in your skills and abilities, you will get the interview and the job. The summary of qualifications yells it out—"You need me!" And the employer yells back—"Yes, I do. Tell me more!"

You will write three, four, or perhaps as many as five bullets which highlight your accomplishments, presenting an overview to the employer of strong, valuable, desirable skills. That is, in essence, what a summary of qualifications is written for. As I say to my clients, it's that simple — and that difficult.

Read all of the examples, whether they are related to your profession or not. You will quickly understand how to approach your own work and life history and write statements about your important abilities.

Remember, each part of the résumé is building more and more interest and getting the reader to the point of saying "Gee, I think this person has qualities that would make for a natural fit with our position. I think I'll call and set up an interview." The résumé cannot lose its impact at any point. If you've got a great job objective and your summary of qualifications reads poorly, you are in trouble. Think about the following examples and why the employer would maintain an interest in our job hunter.

▶ *Special Note*

A Summary of Qualifications takes some time to put together in an effective, award-winning manner. Read through all of the examples and make notes of your own strengths that an employer would find impressive. Also, remember to write the strongest point first, followed by the next strongest point, and so forth. Whether you like it or not — Sell! Sell! Sell! Your future depends on it.

Accountant

- Big six public accounting firm experience with specific exposure to High Tech, Biotech, and Manufacturing industries.
- Successful completion of the Uniform CPA Exam, certification granted 1991.
- Significant and recognized accomplishments; selected to contribute to three project teams to streamline corporate operations.

Accountant

- Three years of solid educational and practical background in all phases of accounting and staff training.
- Experience with multi-fund and complex computerized systems.
- High academic honors; 3.85/4.00 GPA in major.

Administrative Assistant

- Over 15 years offering proven administrative support to high level staff and management teams.
- Ability to work effectively in a team setting or independently, interact with clients and all levels of staff, and complete assignments within defined guidelines.
- Experienced with IBM and Macintosh computers; strong knowledge of WordPerfect 5.0, Microsoft Word 5.0, Lotus 1-2-3, and graphic software applications.

Administrative Support

- Over 5 years of proven administrative support skills, successfully working with staff, clients, and various agencies.
- Experienced dealing with all levels of management and meeting set goals.
- Seeing each assignment through to a successful completion according to supervisory requirements.
- Strong interpersonal skills with creative problem-solving abilities.

Advertising/Promotions

- Strong background in promotions, advertising, and merchandising, supported by distinguished academic performance.
- Expertise in marketing targeted consumer products, including sportswear, leisure clothing, and related athletic equipment.
- Proven ability in training staff to reach corporate-defined goals while staying within

prescribed budgets.

Architectural Designer

- Five years progressive, practical architectural experience for a leading area firm.
- Consistent record of achievement, using technical and creative skills to complete projects ahead of schedule and within budget.
- Analytical and decision making abilities; respected team member.

Artist/Art Teacher

- Professional experience teaching adults and children various art techniques, with specialization in figurative painting and drawing.
- Successful in developing and nurturing the creativity and imagination of the individual.
- Participation in over 15 national and international solo and group shows.
- Recipient of numerous awards and commissions, as well as inclusion in many private collections.

Banker

- Nine years of banking experience, with primary responsibility for managing a diversified portfolio of troubled commercial loans.
- Expertise and industry knowledge in production and marketing, construction materials manufacturing, and a variety of other retailing operations.
- Substantial bankruptcy experience including relief motions, debtor-in-possession financing, and the evaluation and development of reorganization/liquidation plans in both Chapter 11 and 7 proceedings.

Banker

- Twelve years experience in banking with expertise in consumer lending.
- A solid record of achievement in streamlining operations to increase efficiency.
- Introducing new services to increase profitability; building market share with no additions to staff.
- Successfully collaborating with managers at all corporate levels.

Banking/Employee Benefits

- Ten years experience in employee benefits, offering expertise in large account benefits consulting and account management.
- Comprehensive knowledge of products through six years of directing the Benefits Development Department.
- Proven ability to introduce and implement products to major customers.
- Team building and leadership skills.

Banquet Manager

- Manage in-house banquet facilities and increase revenues substantially over the short term.
- Perform all assignments successfully, resulting in five promotions in seven years.
- Establish effective human relations with all staff and management to create highly energetic teams.
- Attend business seminars to acquire added expertise in restaurant operations.

Bartender/Waiter

- Act as host, wine steward and tableside preparer for exclusive downtown restaurant
- Prepare and serve salads, specialty coffees and flambés.
- Bartend for corporate functions. Inventory liquor, stock bar, prepare drinks and oversee all bartending operations.
- Wait on tables during absence of needed crew.
- T.I.P. Certified/Alcohol Intervention Method (1990).

Bookkeeper

- Excellent organizational, time management, and communication skills.
- Ability to perform accurately in high pressure situations.
- Knowledge of Lotus 1-2-3 and Paradox computer programs, creating and maintaining expense and income spreadsheets.
- Extensive coursework in bookkeeping and accounting.
- Typing at 50+ wpm.

Bookstore Manager/College Textbooks

- Three years experience as textbook manager with hands on involvement in the development of new automated book tracking systems.
- Assisting professors with textbook orders and decisions.
- Experience developing improved customer relations, used book programs, and streamlined operational functions.

Business Administration

- High academic honors; graduating in top 10% of class, while maintaining a 30+ hour work week.
- Responsible for financing 100% of educational and living costs.
- Excellent computer skills with both Macintosh and IBM computers and various software applications.
- Ability to lead team efforts and meet corporate goals.

Career Counselor

- Trained in career counseling to professionals and recent college graduates.
- Knowledgeable of local businesses and non-profits, as well as agencies and their methodology for recruiting and hiring staff.
- Ability to interpret assessment instruments Myers-Briggs Type Indicator (MBTI) as well as the Harrington/O'Shea Career Decision Making System (CDM).
- Knowledgeable in resume writing, job searching, and interviewing techniques.
- Strong research and writing abilities.

Chef's Assistant

- Academic training and a willingness to learn new cooking skills needed by an innovative chef.
- Numerous cooking classes, with extensive training by respected chefs.
- Participation in 3 special cooking programs in France and Italy to develop added skills.

Clinician

- Experienced manager with excellent business, academic, and clinical credentials.
- Strong record of building effective teams and promoting company objectives in fast-changing environments.
- Highly skilled at identifying problems and creating successful solutions.
- Successful at prioritizing work and involving customers in needs assessments and resolutions.
- Recognized for empowering staff and encouraging varied methods of responsibility reporting.

Community Volunteer

- Over five years of academic and practical training with the deaf community.
- Member of the following organizations associated with the deaf community: MSAD, NAD, and READY.
- Presently living with a deaf woman, developing signing skills and gaining direct experience with a member of the deaf community.
- American Sign Language classes: New Jersey State Association for the Deaf (ASL I); private classes.

Computer Sales

- Successful marketing and sales representative with over six years of proven sales skills requiring detailed demonstrations of products and commitment to customer support.

•Highly motivated with experience in coordinating client base needs with corporate strategies, researching best cost strategies, and supporting clients with installation, in depth training, and follow-up support.

•Proven ability to demonstrate appropriate reasons for upgrading systems and software using IBM-based product lines.

•Solid closing track record.

Construction

•Construction expertise: writing proposals, creating and delivering presentations, and performing public relations campaigns for banks and public agencies.

•Solid sales and marketing experience, aggressively developing strategies to achieve and surpass revenue goals.

•Excellent interpersonal skills, effectively instituting long-term and stable client relationships.

•Computer literate professional successful at providing tracking reports highlighting projections and results.

Coordinator/Medical Services

•Over 8 years administration experience in the medical field, offering support to doctors and nurses as a Unit Coordinator.

•Extensive supervisory and training experience with new staff.

•Coordinator of patient-care activities with other departments in hospital.

•Excellent medical terminology knowledge, as well as effective interpersonal and leadership abilities.

Counselor

•Ability to supervise mental health counseling staff, including the initial screening and hiring process.

•Experience as a mental health counselor with direct responsibility for developing treatment programs.

•Direct experience counseling clients in clinical settings using proven problem solving methods of treatment.

•Propose strategies toward the development of client creativity and verbal skills development.

•Effective in the development and implementation of innovative programs.

Customer Service Representative

•Ability to successfully manage multiple assignments and priorities.

•Highly developed analytical and problem solving skills.

•Outstanding customer service skills.

•Ability to work independently and as a member of a team.

•Highly motivated and goal directed

•Arrive at the highest quality in all projects undertaken.

Customer Service Representative

•Very effective within interpersonal contact situations.

•Good listening skills with a receptive and personable style.

•Ability to maintain a focus on total customer service in complex and ambiguous situations.

•Dependable, enthusiastic, and results oriented.

Day Care Worker

•Twelve years experience teaching toddlers and preschoolers in nursery school and day care settings.

•Patient, focused, and committed to working with children.

•Self-motivated and creative with the ability to work independently and as part of a group.

•Communicate with parents in a friendly, diplomatic fashion.

•Overall sense of responsibility.

Elementary Teacher

•Proven skills in program development for children of multicultural families.

•Experience working with special needs programs for children.

•Leader in problem resolution, parent-teacher conferences, and consultation to families of at risk children.

•Organize and coordinate curriculum and design classroom settings to ensure success.

•Establish training focused on issues of discipline, stress, and family relationship issues.

•Full understanding and compliance with agency regulations.

Entry Level Manager

•Proven experience in management, working in service industries and retail sales.

•Providing the best in customer service.

•Fluency in Spanish.

•Working full time while attending college.

Executive Assistant

- Proven ability to offer primary support to a management team, working effectively in project management assignments in such areas as fundraising and special promotions.

- Results-oriented, organized, and able to work in a team environment to complete projects on time and within budget.

Financial Services Representative

- Highly motivated executive with 8 years in the financial services industry, specializing in investor relations, business management, and financial administration.

- Strong negotiation expertise and excellent oral and written communication skills.

- Expertise in building and managing diverse relationships across all levels of management and functional areas.

Food Service Manager

- Four years of solid experience in highly rated hotel restaurants.

- Proven expertise in hotel restaurant management working with European chefs.

- Strong knowledge of modern management design in national and international markets.

Hospitality Manager

- Hospitality manager with over 5 years experience coordinating personnel according to guest expectations.

- Excellent track record developing streamlined operations while contributing to profitability.

- Known for innovative leadership which increases employee productivity.

Human Resource Administrator

- Widely experienced in all phases of Human Resources Administration — writing and implementing policies and procedures, employee and labor relations, and acting as liaison to executive management.

- More than 14 years expertise in the banking and financial services industries.

Insurance Executive

- Over seven years of leadership in the insurance industry.

- Developing revenue-building products and building long term marketing and profit strategies.

- Dealing with hospitals, physicians, and corporate clients; negotiating contracts, interpreting existing plan documents, and achieving cost containment requirements.

•Excellent high level presentation skills.

Interior Designer

•Professional and academic training in space planning, window treatments and interior design.

•Successful conversion of an 8,000+ square foot retail space.

•Willingness to work overtime to meet aggressive deadlines.

•Excellent interpersonal skills, articulate and empathetic, great personality, and very motivated.

International Marketing

•Over 15 years in international marketing and operations, with proven experience developing new markets and corporate relationships.

•Recognized as a leader in introducing innovative merchandise and maintaining product quality.

•Multilingual, with extensive training in and practical experience using four languages.

Kitchen Worker

•Six years of proven kitchen experience, providing consistent, conscientious, high quality food preparation in fast-paced kitchen environments.

•Strong industry knowledge combined with a dedicated work ethic and commitment to providing exceptional service.

•Pursuit of an Associates degree in Business Administration to add value to an employer; one semester until completion.

Lab Assistant/Intern

•Proven experience as a lab assistant, offering strengths in environmental monitoring and validation.

•Excellent research and writing abilities, writing reports and complying with industry regulatory standards.

•Computer literate using IBM and Macintosh applications.

Legislative Aide

•Aggressive professional with experience in planning agendas, presentations and public speaking, and ad campaign development.

•Ability to learn new systems and procedures quickly.

•Client relation and problem solving abilities.

•Computer literate with both Macintosh and IBM computers.

Liquor Sales

- Broad knowledge of the retail liquor industry including all aspects of purchasing, pricing, and inventory control.
- Proven management skills working with sales representatives, clients, and personnel.
- Five years of proven success in retail promotions, banking procedures, payroll deposits, and various administrative tasks.

Maintenance Supervisor

Proven experience working for commercial properties, with knowledge of:
- Electrical Wiring
- Domestic and Commercial Refrigeration
- Residential and Auto Air Conditioning
- Refrigerant Handling
- Gauge Procedures
- Charging and Evacuation of Systems
- Ice Makers and Water Coolers
- Refrigeration/Electric Codes

Maintenance Supervisor

- Over 12 years of management experience in maintenance, with proven success at supervising staff and ensuring high quality standards.
- Reporting to building owners/developers with documentation supporting the staff's adherence to company operational standards.
- Performing duties within budget and meeting all deadlines.
- Continual enhancement of skills through classes, seminars, and special company projects.

Marketing Coordinator

- Proven expertise in marketing; writing detailed proposals, creating catalogs and brochures, delivering presentations, and building teams to realize goals.
- Achieve and surpass revenue goals and maintain leadership position amongst competitors.
- Excellent interpersonal skills, effectively instituting programs which ensure long-term and stable client relationships.
- Oversee billing and reporting systems to comply with departmental budgets.
- Hire and train staff where teamwork and quality assurance are given primary importance.

Media Spot Buyer

- Proven success developing media objectives and strategies for large corporations, utilizing over eight years of professional experience in the field.
- Take charge individual with expertise in buying cable, spot television, and radio, as well as coordinating special promotional events.
- Perform research and analytical studies to demonstrate effective use of media campaign budgets.

Merchandising Executive

- Highly motivated, analytical team player with 12+ years of experience in coordinating 40+ staff, researching best cost methods of delivery, and supporting key individuals in order to meet corporate goals.
- Proven ability to establish vendor contacts where quality, cost, response and delivery efficiencies, and overall service standards meet stringent corporate requirements.
- Expertise in building and managing product lines.

MIS Administrator/Financial Services

- Over 15 years of proven systems leadership, supporting the objectives and goals of senior management and directors.
- Executive officer with responsibilities for professional staff servicing 4,300 accounts valued over $10 billion.
- Knowledge of equity and fixed income investments, SEC reporting requirements, and bank operations.
- Team leader in charge of systems decentralization, initiating projects to reduce costs and maximize efficiencies.

Musician - Personal Statement

- Born in Tokyo, Japan and raised in New York.
- Began studying percussion in 1977 at the age of 8. Trained on concert snare drum, timpani, and drumset.
- Within one year, began performing in city/county bands and orchestras.
- Moved to Hong Kong in 1980 and began studying at Hong Kong International School. Played in concert bands, the orchestra, jazz bands, and small "club-date" bands. Received Award for Excellence in Jazz.
- After 5 years of study in Hong Kong, moved back to New York to attend the New York School of the Arts.
- Participated in jazz bands, jazz combos, the Orchestra, the Concert Band, and in studio recordings.
- Member of New York Youth Philharmonic

- Member of New York All-State Honor Band
- Member of New York All-State Honor Orchestra
- Moved to Boston to receive degree from Berklee College of Music.
- Active training and development of skills with extensive private instruction.

Mutual Fund Analyst

- Design and market computer-based mutual fund reports which enable management to set corporate strategies.
- In-depth knowledge of competitor pricing, performance, and policies.
- Proven success at writing reports used by executive board and marketing group to effectively sell products and increase market share.
- Research products and negotiate with outside vendors to purchase systems which positively impact division.

Office Assistant

- Solid experience with all types of word processing and data entry assignments.
- Detail oriented with ability to see tasks through to completion.
- Strong organizational and interpersonal skills.

Operations Manager

- Expertise in communications, public relations, negotiations, and staff training and development.
- Ability to cultivate quality staff for project teams needed to streamline existing systems and operations.
- Manage project coordination, communications, and staff functions.
- Troubleshoot and develop operations to maximize profits.

Personnel Manager

- Outstanding ability in personnel interviewing and skills assessment.
- Strong interpersonal and communication skills.
- Equally effective working independently or as part of a team.
- Sharp, poised; able to convey a professional image.
- Broad educational and cultural background; active involvement in inner city projects; fluency in Spanish.

Product Development Manager

- Entrepreneurial approach to creating new markets for health care products.
- Successful track record in proposing and implementing new product opportunities that generate substantial revenues.

- Design marketing/sales strategies to advance market share.
- A hands-on marketing manager respected by staff and project teams.

Program Development

- Over 11 years of proven program development and planning experience in the health service field.
- Expertise in public and media relations, fund raising, and marketing.
- Successful recruitment, training, and evaluation of high level staff.
- Ability to conceptualize and implement research programs and write grants to gain necessary funding.

Programmer/Project Analyst

Programmer with excellent listening skills, an imaginative nature, and resourceful character when getting management to deliver specifications according to set schedules.

Real Estate Construction - Site Manager

- Over 15 years of commercial construction experience, with excellent mechanical aptitude and willingness to follow designated practices and procedures.
- Foreman experience, directing efforts of crew in all site areas.
- Proven ability to perform and oversee heavy physical work in all seasons.

Real Estate Sales

- Over 10 years of success in every aspect of real estate sales, including commercial and residential, existing and new construction, with overall career sales exceeding $45 million.
- A solid track record in negotiating and working with developers, lenders, attorneys, and prospective clients.
- Expertise in reading, qualifying, and closing prospective deals.

Realtor

- Over nine years of demonstrated expertise in the marketing, financing, and negotiating of commercial and residential real estate.
- A strong track record assisting with the acquisition and disposition of multi-million dollar properties and developments.
- Extensive experience managing a large sales force.

Recruiter/Trainer

- Responsible for overall training programs for 800 front-line staff.
- Leader in the effective screening of approximately 4,000 applicants in two major

recruitment drives.

•Participated in labor negotiations culminating in major work process re-engineering without affecting work output.

•Established training facility to fulfill contractual obligations to outside clients.

Refrigeration Technician

Technical Summary: Over 11 years of experience in:

•Commercial Refrigeration

•Domestic Refrigeration and Room Air Conditioning

•Refrigeration Wiring

•Installation of Draught Beer and Wire Lines

•Gas Furnace Repairs

Restaurant Manager

•Communicate information clearly to all staff members.

•Adapt to various situations with the ability to utilize available resources.

•Solve problems with inventive and creative approaches.

•Excellent interpersonal skills and tremendous physical stamina.

Restaurant Manager

•Proven leader in area restaurants with a track record of revitalizing franchises.

•Breadth of experience in all facets of restaurant operations: inventories, labor, food costs, and cash handling.

•Excellent planning, leadership, customer relation, and interpersonal abilities.

Restaurant Manager/Event Planner

•An effective leader with strong qualifications and over 10 years of experience in restaurant/service businesses.

•Setting priorities to achieve management goals on time and within budget.

•Detail oriented with proven ability to organize all details of an event from conception to completion.

•Strong interpersonal and communications skills, dealing effectively with corporate and individual clients as well as all levels of staff.

Retail Manager

•Effective leadership of staff members, promoting teamwork and goal setting.

•Maintaining highest levels of customer service, tracking client purchases and developing long-term relationships.

- Supervisory skills in all facets of store operations, including payroll, scheduling, client mailings, opening and closing, and dealing with merchandisers.
- Understanding the retail buying process, setting strategies which promote company growth.

Retail Manager

- Six years of managerial experience
- Three years of retail management
- Skilled in training and recruiting key personnel
- Strong verbal and written communication skills

Retail Sales/Fashion

- Total of four years experience in men's clothing, with over $350,000 in last year's annual sales output.
- Current with ongoing fashion trends both nationally and internationally.
- Background in design/display with academic honors in fashion merchandising.
- Multicultural, multilingual.

Sales/Corporate Leasing

- Generating high returns, in sales and profit, for company.
- Learning the priorities of clients, assessing current and future building needs, and realizing long term and stable corporate relationships.
- Spotting new trends and introducing new and updated products to the marketplace.
- Resolving client concerns and problems with a partnership approach to their needs.
- Establishing new business relationships that generate solid results to corporate revenues.

Sales Manager

- Eight years of sales management experience with a solid record of achieving and surpassing company goals.
- Successful training, development, and leadership of staff.
- Excellent written and verbal communication skills.
- Advanced analysis skills coupled with extensive use of Lotus 1-2-3 and Microsoft Windows.

Salesperson

- Extensive sales and marketing experience, regularly achieving top salesperson position.

• Aggressive development of assigned accounts, with monthly average increases for territories from $32,000 to $45,000.

• Proven ability to manage salespeople, with responsibility for managing up to 5 support staff.

• Excellent interpersonal skills, effectively instituting long-term and stable client relationships which help maintain and surpass revenue goals.

Secretary

• Extensive reception and secretarial experience

• Proven skills in typing, bookkeeping, and office management

• Technical proficiency with both IBM and Macintosh computers, including Lotus 1-2-3, WordPerfect, and Microsoft Word

Social Worker

• Excellent problem solving and counseling skills.

• Demonstrated ability in adolescent needs assessment.

• Valued as a contributing member of an interdisciplinary team.

• Deep compassion and commitment in helping adolescents.

• Sensitivity to cultural and ethnic issues.

Supervisor

Nine years management/supervisory experience including:

• Strong record of achieving and surpassing company sales goals.

• Successful training, development, and leadership of staff.

• Strong interpersonal and decision-making skills.

• Extensive knowledge of retail in high end markets, with excellent marketing skills needed to attract long term clients.

Telemarketer

• Recognized as a leader in telemarketing sales, consistently surpassing all defined quotas.

• Close 60 to 70 deals per month to exceed quota requirements.

• Consistently surpass requirements and attain highest call/close ratio in company.

• Ability to work independently, generate leads, and close according to an organization's revenue goals.

Telemarketing Manager

• Over 4 years of proven business experience requiring strong telemarketing and communication skills.

- Highly motivated with a desire to learn new skills and contribute to management goals and objectives.
- Effective team player with the ability to finish projects on deadline.
- Computer literate, performing all types of processing functions to update client files on-line.

Television Production

- 10+ years experience working in the television field.
- Hardworking, reliable, flexible, and a team player; successfully meet pressure-filled nightly deadlines.
- Broad knowledge of various equipment used in television production.
- Strong oral and written communication skills.

Theatre Art Director

- Proven ability to work with agency art directors, producers, and others to develop storyboards, from both a conceptual and budgetary point of view.
- Contract with vendors such as set builders and decorators, wardrobers, scenic designers, and special effects personnel to meet production needs.
- Establish work schedules, arrange pick-ups and deliveries, and oversee all projects through to completion.

Trainer/Teacher

Highly motivated with 6+ years of proven experience in the areas of staff training and leadership. Energetic, management-oriented professional with excellent record of growth and accomplishment. Strong appreciation for superlative human resource management services.

Travel Planner

- Over six years experience in custom designing travel itineraries.
- Comprehensive knowledge of tour operations management, telemarketing, and customer service.
- Substantial experience in European markets and training personnel in all aspects of international travel.

Volunteer

- Proven ability to deal effectively with a wide range of people from various cultures and socioeconomic environments.
- Effective problem-solver, dealing with difficult situations and working them through to a successful resolution.
- Teaching new skill sets to people from different backgrounds.

Sometimes, the summary of qualifications provides enough of your general credentials for the employer to decide on setting up the interview. At the very least, the summary should be powerful enough to move the reader to the next category. Remember, the reader must be thinking "yes, we need these types of strengths and skills. Tell me more!"

WORK EXPERIENCE

▼
AKA's:

Professional Experience	*Experience*	*Business Experience*
Internships	*Achievements*	*Professional Background*
Technical Experience	*Volunteer Experience*	*Past Experience*
History	*Career History*	*Community Service*
Leadership Experience	*Professional History*	*Professional Accomplishments*
Systems Experience	*Freelance Assignments*	*Government Contracts*
Personal Background	*Part-Time Work*	*Medical Experience*
Music Projects	*Agency Assignments*	

Just the facts, ma'am. Wouldn't it be nice to just present the facts and be done with it? Why all the fuss? Here are my skills. Give me the job. Simple?

Time to wake up and smell the coffee.

Think of it this way. For a job that you'll stay with for a few years, most employers will be paying out well over $100,000. If you were paying out that kind of money for a product, wouldn't you want to know about any defects, whether it can work for long periods of time without breaking down, and if it fits in with the rest of your decor?

Your work experience represents you. You chose your work history. We live in a democratic society which allows you to make your own choices, for better or worse. Your résumé and work experience are brief autobiographies. Make the employer want to meet the author. You.

▶ *To split or not to split...*

Recently, we had a young woman come into our offices. She wanted to pursue a career in radio broadcasting. Her dream is to be a successful on-air personality. But we had a small problem. While she had considerable experience in college radio, she had been out of school, and radio, for 2 years and was working as an administrative assistant at a pharmaceutical company.

The radio credentials were impressive. She'd hosted her own programs, done research work for well-known on-air personalities, and even set-up special events and coordinated promo giveaways for various holidays. And more. So how would we reconcile her talents and desires with her current occupation?

The answer was to split her work experience.

We created 2 headings applicable to work experience. Simply, they were listed as "RADIO EXPERIENCE" and "OTHER EXPERIENCE". Thus, we were able to lead off with the experience that would benefit the new employer. After all, performing the duties of an administrative assistant is a great skill, but the radio exposure will probably pull more interest to the radio station.

Remember, you have approximately 30 seconds to tell your story. You do not want an employer spending the first 20 seconds just getting to the parts applicable to their needs! Why limit yourself to only 5 or 10 seconds? Also, our radio announcer can list her dates of employment so the employer can readily see when certain work assignments were performed. I believe dates are important relevant to specific work experiences. And that is why I don't like functional résumés.

▶ *Functional Versus Chronological*

Some books advocate using functional résumés to sell your strengths. This type of résumé lists the things you have done but does not relate the accomplishments to specific jobs you have held. Another popular résumé book in the market suggests a functional résumé is the only way to go. I think, however, that there are many negative factors related to the functional versions.

You may build up experience that the employer is looking for, but to ask the employer to figure out when you did what may not be worth her trouble. For example, if we need a problem-solver to fix our widget program, and you seem to offer the needed skills but your employment listings "kinda, sorta" suggest you did what we need, but perhaps back in the 1970s, will you help me get the job done TODAY? If not misleading, a functional résumé is at least confusing to the reader. When did you do it? How long have you been doing it for? The employer may very well say — "Oh, forget it. This isn't worth my time." Remember, the job applicant pool is huge. You only have seconds to sell your strengths. Don't make the employer figure out your credentials. There are too many other résumés ready to compete with yours.

▶ *Action Verbs*

Action verbs help make your point quickly. Instead of saying "I was responsible for getting the group together to discuss our sales plans for the month," why not use the following:

"Organized weekly meetings for team members to set sales strategies."

An action verb energizes the thought and makes the reader feel the action taking place. I think these words work because they create visual pictures. You can see someone who has "trained" new employees or "directed" the sales team; you don't get much visually for someone "responsible for" a project or assignment.

Now, on to the list. In my other book, The Smart Job Search, I listed action verbs and people asked for more, more, more! As requested, here are many more action verbs:

accelerated	adapted	advised
accepted	added	aided
accompanied	addressed	alerted
accomplished	adjusted	allocated
accounted for	administered	allotted
achieved	adopted	alphabetized
acquired	advanced	amended
acted	advertised	amplified

analyzed	changed	coordinated
anchored	charted	copied
announced	checked	copyrighted
answered	chose	corrected
anticipated	clarified	corresponded
appeared	classified	counseled
applied	cleared	counted
appointed	cleared up	crafted
appraised	closed	created
approved	coached	critiqued
arbitrated	collaborated	dealt
argued	collected	debated
arranged	combined	debugged
articulated	commended	decided
assembled	communicated	decreased
assessed	compared	defined
assigned	competed	delegated
assisted	compiled	delivered
assumed	completed	demonstrated
assured	composed	described
attained	computed	designed
attended	conceived	detailed
audited	conceptualized	detected
auditioned	concluded	determined
authored	condensed	developed
authorized	conditioned	devised
awarded	conducted	diagnosed
balanced	conferred	diagrammed
bargained	confirmed	digested
began	conserved	diminished
bolstered	consolidated	directed
briefed	constructed	disciplined
broadcasted	consulted	discovered
brought	contacted	discussed
budgeted	continued	displayed
built	contracted	distributed
calculated	contributed	documented
casted	controlled	drafted
catalogued	converted	dramatized
caught	conveyed	drew up
caused	convinced	dropped
chaired	cooperated	earned

edited
educated
effected
elaborated
elected
elicited
eliminated
emphasized
employed
encouraged
enforced
engineered
enhanced
enjoyed
enlarged
enlisted
ensured
entered
entertained
established
estimated
evaluated
examined
exceeded
excelled
executed
exercised
expanded
expedited
experimented
explained
explored
expressed
extinguished
extracted
facilitated
familiarized
filed
financed
fixed
focused
forecasted

foresaw
formulated
fortified
forwarded
fostered
found
founded
freelanced
furnished
furthered
gained
gathered
gave
generated
governed
graded
greeted
grossed
guided
handled
harmonized
hastened
heightened
helped
highlighted
hiked
hired
hosted
housed
hunted
identified
illustrated
implemented
improved
improvised
included
incorporated
increased
indicated
individualized
influenced
informed

initiated
innovated
inspected
inspired
installed
instilled
instituted
instructed
insured
integrated
interacted
interpreted
intervened
interviewed
introduced
invented
inventoried
investigated
involved
issued
joined
kept
labored
launched
learned
lectured
led
licensed
listened
litigated
lobbied
located
looked
made
maintained
managed
mapped out
mastered
maximized
measured
mediated
memorized

mentored	presented	reported
met	presided	represented
modeled	prevailed	rescued
modified	prevented	researched
monitored	processed	reserved
motivated	produced	resolved
moved	programmed	responded
named	projected	restored
narrated	promoted	restructured
negotiated	pronounced	resulted in
netted	proofed	retained
observed	proofread	returned
obtained	proposed	revamped
offered	proved	revealed
opened	provided	reviewed
operated	publicized	revised
ordered	published	rewarded
organized	purchased	rotated
originated	put	said
outlined	qualified	sampled
overcame	quickened	satisfied
overhauled	ran	saved
oversaw	realized	saw
paid	received	scheduled
painted	recommended	scouted
participated	reconciled	screened
perceived	recorded	scripted
performed	recruited	scrutinized
permitted	rectified	searched
persuaded	reduced	secured
photographed	referred	selected
pinpointed	registered	sent
pioneered	regulated	served
placed	rehabilitated	set
planed	reinforced	set up
planned	related	settled
played	rendered	shaped
policed	renewed	shared
portrayed	renovated	shipped
practiced	reorganized	shored up
predicted	repaired	showed
prepared	replaced	sifted

simplified	submitted	trained
smoothed	suggested	transferred
sold	summarized	transformed
solved	supervised	translated
sorted	supplied	transmitted
sought	supported	traveled
spearheaded	surmounted	treated
specialized	surpassed	tutored
specified	surveyed	typed
spoke	systematized	typed
standardized	tabulated	uncovered
stated	targeted	unearthed
stopped	taught	updated
straightened	tested	upped
streamlined	tightened	utilized
strengthened	took over	welcomed
stripped	totaled	won
structured	toured	worked
studied	tracked	wrote

Your work experience should give highlighted details of your past performance in relation to what potential employers need in a great employee. If, back in 1981, you were the best darn typist in the entire division, but the new employer discarded their last typewriter 3 years ago to only use Macintosh computers, your ability will at best be considered a supporting strength. Will they want to train you? Can they find someone who offers solid Macintosh experience?

How do you find out what employers need? Research. Research. And more research. You have a vast array of support services available to you. As I said in my last book, one of the greatest places to begin your search is with your public library. You can find listings of area companies, business journals that identify segments of businesses and provide details of future corporate strategies, and books dealing with areas you might be interested in for YOUR future.

Of course, use the expertise of the librarian! Your librarian is the greatest resource to you when you walk through that front door. An example should prove that, no matter what the field, you can find innumerable leads using the library.

At Smart Résumés, I met with a client who specialized in Geodesy and Cartography. Simply put, his professional life was centered around making maps! I don't know about you, but I didn't envision much of a market for his wonderful talents. Boy, was I wrong! And fascinated by what he found.

Through library research, he was subsequently able to contact over 125 firms, in Massachusetts alone, who were in the business of or had divisions for making maps! When you start to think about city planning, roads, bridges, townships, private properties, subdivisions of land parcels, the U.S. government's tracking of everything — the list could go on and on, I came to realize how extensive and important Geodesy and Cartography really are to the way we live.

So if you are a bank manager, a hotel administrator, an advertising person, etc. — remember, a man who makes maps found 125 companies to approach. In one state! Dozens, hundreds, and more contacts are available to you if you conduct research. <u>Research is the key.</u>

When you write about your professional, volunteer, and other types of work experiences, think of short, strong "action" statements that convey the great things you have done. I often use bulleted statements over paragraphs of information. Again, remember you have less than a minute to sell your whole work and life history! Three, four, or five bulleted statements can be read easily and quickly.

It is acceptable to use paragraph formats on your résumé. If you do, though, remember to make them short and powerful. Two paragraphs, each half a page in length, simply won't get read.

Once again, I recommend you read through all the work experiences, even if many don't seem to fit in with your work and life history. Through the examples, you will quickly understand how to create powerful statements about your own accomplishments.

Here they are:

Academia/Department Head

1981 - 1987   **Department Head, Foreign Language Department**
                     Regency High School, Lexington, KY

- Supervised and evaluated 17 staff members in high school and 2 middle schools
- Directed history programs for 1450 students
- Formulated and executed annual department budgets
- Developed, implemented, and evaluated curricula
- Conducted annual pre-registration surveys and subsequent registrations
- Recruited, organized, and conducted annual foreign travel-study group tours to Europe (classroom extension)

Architectural Designer

ALICE MUNROE DESIGN GROUP, Muncie, IN   5/87 - 1/89
Designer/Drafter

- Contributed to design of new construction, residential renovation and millwork detailing. Managed client review meetings, prepared design development drawings, as well as bid and construction documents, presentation drawings, model building, and the coordination with contractors and engineers.

Work includes:

13 Taylor Street, Talma, IN
782 Teegarden Court, Staunton, IN

14A Howard Avenue, Muncie, IN

Bookkeeper

SHOALS, VERNON & JONES, INC. New York, NY
Accounts Payable Manager (11/88 - 2/93)
- Managed all facets of accounts payable department, including the coordination of all payment schedules and maintenance of customer relations
- Handled daily cash-flow analysis statements.
- Assisted in preparation of financial statements and closings on a monthly basis.
- Supervised all aspects of company payroll.

Clinical Intern

Internal Medicine (1990)
- Department of Internal Medicine at Harlem Hospital Center, New York.

Cardiac Surgery (1991)
- Department of Cardiac Surgery at Mount Sinai Medical Center, New York.

Emergency Medicine (1990 - 1992)
- Department of Internal Medicine (Emergency Unit) at Metropolitan Hospital Center, New York.

Anesthesiology (1990 - 1992)
- Department of Anesthesiology at Metropolitan Hospital Center, New York.

Clinical Intern

MEMPHIS OPTOMETRIC CENTER, Memphis, TN   1987 - 1988
An interdisciplinary primary care facility with emphasis on refraction, binocularity, and ocular health assessment.

GERMANTOWN LENS CENTER, Germantown, TN   1988
Provided patients with contact lens evaluations, fittings, and follow-up care.

College Debating Coach

RHODES COLLEGE, Memphis, TN   9/92 - 12/92
Responsibilities included assisting college debaters with constructing and competing in intercollegiate competitions.

Community/Academic Services

LOYOLA COLLEGE ALUMNI OFFICE, Baltimore, MD
Phonathon Worker. Conducted telephone calls to Alumni to raise money for the

Building Fund.

AIDS ACTION COMMITTEE, Baltimore, MD
Volunteer. Provided support and assisted in group activities with primary responsibility for writing press releases and articles for monthly newsletter.

Consultant

TEXAS SOUTHERN UNIVERSITY, Houston, TX   1990 - Present
Development Group   (Part-Time)
Consultant
Consulted with clients in the Texas region with existing or future businesses, developing marketing plans and feasibility studies and involving all aspects of business education — accounting, marketing, economics, etc.

Insurance Agent

THE NEW ENGLAND, Boston, MA

1990 - 1993

Technical Specialist
- Investigate, evaluate, and negotiate general liability claims and serious injury cases in commercial lines unit. Monitor litigation process and determine which cases should be settled rather than tried. Handle products liability cases up to $1,000,000 in exposure.

- Prepare status reports. Draft and finalize reserve advisory and requests for authority letters to risk managers of national accounts. Conduct mediations and binding arbitrations. Attend depositions and trials.

- Successfully implemented special project designed to reduce litigation expenses by identifying and resolving cases warranting settlement. Initiate and conduct settlement days with plaintiff firms. Communicate regularly with staff and panel counsel, claims personnel, and plaintiff's bar.

Intern

Ecole de Cuisine Bouché, Paris, France
- Completed 6-week intense professional training program. Studied classic French cuisine, pastry and chocolate, contemporary and regional cooking.

Librarian

NEW ENGLAND CONSERVATORY OF MUSIC, Boston, MA
Head Librarian, 1985 - 1988
Duties included ordering and cataloging new materials, preserving historical items, training and supervising student workers, giving class instruction on library use,

answering reference questions, and participating in meetings of area music librarians.

THE JULIARD SCHOOL, New York, NY
Reference Librarian, 1983 - 1984
Evening reference librarian for conservatory library. Answered reference questions and supervised student circulation staff.

Law Associate

LEVY, POLLOCK & GOLDMAN, Los Angeles, CA
Associate, Corporate Department, 6/91 to Present
Summer Associate, Summer 1990
Assigned to Mergers and Acquisitions Practice Group. Researched commercial law issues, conducted due diligence reviews, and drafted and negotiated primary and ancillary agreements and documents in connection with acquisitions and   dispo tions of U.S. and foreign corporations in $30 to $100 million range.

Drafted documents relating to other transactions (general corporate, real estate, lending) and provided research and brief/memorandum writing support to Litigation Department in complex commercial litigation context.

Medical Technician

MAGEE-WOMEN'S HOSPITAL, Pittsburgh, PA
Pathology Technician (4/88 - Present)
- Prepared non-gynecological specimens in teaching hospital of 210 beds.
- Prepared cells for specialists in the treatment/diagnoses of medical and surgical problems involving approximately 11,000 cases yearly.
- Collaborated with pathologist in creating a computerized software program detailing critical facts needed by hospitals for making critical decisions.
- Updated computerized cytology laboratory procedure manual for specimens received.
- Operated computer to record daily flow of patients' cytology reports.
- Instituted follow-up program on atypical case histories to serve as early warning system to patients for preventing cancer and detecting diseases.

Military Personnel

7/83 - 5/87   **UNITED STATES ARMY**
Sergeant
- Supervised crew of five man fire team. Wrote training outlines and conducted classes on common tasks at platoon and company level. Completed four-week Leadership Development

Course at the Non-Commission Officer Academy.

Awards:
• Army Achievement Medal
• Good Conduct Medal
• Expert Infantryman's Badge
• Air Assault Badge

Nurse

5/89 - Present   **ST. FRANCIS MEMORIAL HOSPITAL, San Francisco, CA**
Critical Care Staff Nurse
Primary nursing care of two critically ill patients (i.e. trauma and all types of immediate post-operative surgical patients). Management of patients with invasive central
lines, cardiac monitors, ventilated on respirators. Follow nursing framework and
prescribed medical regime to restore stability, prevent complications, and achieve
optimal patient health.

Post-Graduate Training

DEPARTMENT OF VETERANS AFFAIRS
MEDICAL CENTER, San Francisco, CA
1988 - 1989
Optometric Resident
Post-graduate training experience in vision care in a multi-disciplinary outpatient
healthcare setting. Duties include low vision examinations of visually impaired veterans, disease evaluation and management, and supervision of fourth year optometry
students.

Producer

FIELD PRODUCER, WNSY - Channel 44, New York, NY   1991 - Present
Produced a wide variety of foreign and domestic stories for this nightly
news program. Assignments included political coverage of Serbian aggression,
breaking news during the first days of the war in Yugoslavia, and a three part
series from Moscow on issues related to the end of Communist rule.

Real Estate Manager

LOS ANGELES DEVELOPMENT PARTNERS   1987 - Present
Director of Leasing
Marketing and leasing retail, industrial, and commercial space, using extensive
knowledge of all facets of real estate including the management, construction,
and financing of commercial buildings. Initially hired as a leasing agent and
subsequently promoted to direct the marketing and leasing efforts for all of

the properties.

- Developed a comprehensive lead referral system utilized by the entire division.
- Led the Commercial Division with the largest amount of transactions completed and space leased.
- Chosen by Senior Management to resolve problems with inactive properties and accounts.
- Consistently raised or maintained the occupancy rate at or above 92% to exceed company's goals.

Realtor

MARKETING REPRESENTATIVE9/91 - 9/92
Boston Realty Group, Boston, MA

- Marketed residential properties to a wide range of clientele. Obtained listings and negotiated terms with landlords and developers.
- Matched clients with properties. Served as liaison between buyer and developer through closing.
- Developed strong communications, negotiations and sales skills.

Reservations Coordinator

GRAND HYATT, New York, NY 1/87 - 10/90
Travel Coordinator

- Coordinated all operational procedures for travel programs as principal liaison between main office and international destinations.
- Controlled inventory in an on-line reservation system to meet the needs of clients while working within the policies of air and hotel contracts.
- Prepared weekly tie-out reports on each destination necessary for proper billing procedures of accounting department.
- Produced weekly client itineraries and packages for airline and overseas representatives.
- Acted as back-up to customer information and reservations departments, providing support during peak cycles.

Retail Manager

PARKER'S, New Orleans, LA   1991 - Present
Manager/Supervisor

Supervised a management staff of eleven. Responsible for all aspects of marketing, merchandising and total store operations for Parker's U.S.A. operations.

Accomplishments:
- Organized and integrated marketing and merchandising strategies for 20 stores.

- Acted as a liaison between buyers and company.
- Forecasted future store and staffing needs and planned and executed projects with managers.
- Ensured flow of merchandise and inventory levels among stores.
- Oversaw all aspects of hiring, training, and placing all managers and management teams throughout the country.
- Responsible for an increase of sales volume of $25 million over three year period.

Student Coordinator

STUDENT COMMUNITY COORDINATOR
Brown University, Providence, RI
Developed campus awareness of community concerns using speakers, campus media, and programs. Organized long-term individual and short-term group   pr jects. Served as liaison between social service agencies and the university.

Teacher

THE WARD SCHOOL, Ward, DE
Teacher Intern (Practicum) — Worked with children in a Resource Room in small groups and one on one. Provided academic and emotional support for children in kindergarten through third grade. Administered Piat-R, Key Math, and Wisspi Design Cards for formal assessments. Participated actively in team meetings, and developing IEP's. (Spring 1993)

WASHINGTON HEIGHTS SCHOOL, Washington Heights, DE
Teacher Intern (Practicum) — Instructed second grade students in spelling, phonics, reading, and math. Developed units and assisted educator in classroom duties. (Fall 1992)

KENT COUNTY ELEMENTARY SCHOOL, Woodbrook, DE
Teacher Intern (Pre-practicum) — Worked one on one and in small groups in an ESL classroom with children in grades first through sixth. Provided support in reading, math, social studies, and science. (Fall 1991)

Teacher

SAN DIEGO SCHOOL SYSTEM, San Diego, CA
Teacher (1991 - Present)
- Determine needs of each child and set up instructional methods based on comprehensive evaluation.
- Prepare evaluations to be submitted to Social Services Department — 1 week initial , 6 month mid-year, and final end-of-year evaluations.
- Conduct daily activities and lessons and analyze progress of each child.
- Submit reports to Education Coordinator, including a weekly activity log and

monthly report specifying goals or program, curriculum development, and classroom needs.

- Maintain proper care of equipment and supplies used daily by children and staff.

Technical Salesperson

THE BOOK RESOURCE, Boston, MA   **10/90 - 3/93**
Sales/Marketing Representative

- Doubled client list during year and a half period with company, achieving a solid 34% closing ratio.
- Demonstrated IBM-based operated systems to booksellers and explained system configuration needs according to business, staff counts, turnover of product lines, and in-store promotions.
- Oversaw systems installations and set up software training programs.
- Worked with corporate technical support teams to incorporate special client specifications requests into system software.
- Attended industry events, including the American Booksellers Association, American Library Association, and other conventions to prospect for new business and present product seminars.

Telemarketer

THE WESTIN PEACHTREE PLAZA, Atlantic, GA   1/92 - Present
Telemarketing Representative

- Preparing reservation and room analysis reports for supervisors.
- Confirming all restaurant and amenities reservations and resolving any discrepancies.
- Working closely with area hosts daily to provide special packages and VIP services.
- Maintaining direct marketing files, including logging, looking up, and confirming reservations.

Tour Director

STUDENT TRAVEL NETWORK, Chicago, IL
Tour Director (1/88 - 8/92)

- Planned, organized, and conducted foreign travel-study tours (adults and school age)
- Developed curricula, reading lists, projects, and support for tour programs
- Negotiated with carriers, travel related services, and tourism agencies
- Facilitated visa and governmental permit processes
- Organized participation in cultural experiences of target countries and target languages

Volunteer

WCVB - Channel 5, Boston, MA
Volunteer camera operator and floor manager for Jimmy Fund Telethon, 1991.

Volunteer

EARTHQUEST, Portland, OR
Non-Profit Organization Volunteer
Working twelve hours per week for non-profit organization; answered telephones, bookkeeping, public relations, and coordinated activities with soup kitchens, homeless shelters, and other non-profit programs in the Washington area.

Volunteer

AIDS ACTION COMMITTEE, New York, NY
Communications Team Member (1992)
Contacting other volunteers to determine availability, special needs, etc.

BETH ISRAEL MEDICAL CENTER, New York, NY
Emergency Room Volunteer (1991)
Delegated duties: Clerical; Messenger; Transport; Patient Care.

NEW YORK ASSOCIATION FOR AIDS CARE
Volunteer — Buddy Program (1991)

Volunteer

MERCY MEDICAL - CARED GIVING CENTER, Denver, CO
Volunteer (1992 - Present)
• Provided respite care to a 5-year old girl with cerebral palsy and mental retardation.
• Assisted in drop-in-center environment with mentally retarded adults.

Volunteer

STARLIGHT FOUNDATION, Portland, ME   3/91 - Present
Area Chairperson
• Serve on committees which grant wishes for children, ages four to seventeen, with critical, chronic, and terminal illnesses.

Our last example shows how someone can give so much to those facing difficult life challenges. Whatever your own challenges, commit to taking care of your own needs and building skills and abilities. Whatever you can do for others has tremendous value. Your résumé is a small snapshot of your life history. Build skills you will always be proud of.

EDUCATION

▼
AKA's:

Educational Honors	*Educational Background*	*Relevant Coursework*
Special Certificates	*Academic Credentials*	*Academic Performance*
Class Projects	*Academic Affiliations*	*Memberships*
Class Organizations		

Certainly, you must have a good education to compete in this high-tech world we live in. But do not for a moment believe that learning skills and abilities comes only with a high-priced "formal education" and not through life experiences.

Everything you do counts as part of your educational process. If you've ever regretted doing some "thing" in life you understand how your past affects your future. Every way you have learned and grown in the past helps determine your future.

Learning and growing. In any context, that is what education is all about.

First, don't limit your definition of an education. Sure, it would be fine to have graduated with high honors from an ivy league college. Does it matter if you only have a high school education? Yes, but only to whatever extent you let it matter and to what level you will compensate with proven skills, abilities, and achievements. Education doesn't end once you have reached a certain age or left a certain classroom.

► ## For the Recent College Graduate

Of course, you will list the name of your college, the city, the state and the year graduated. Also, you will list your particular degree(s) and other concentrations which would benefit an employer.

But what does that information tell the employer? Yes, it suggests a certain level of intellect, perhaps depending upon the school attended or your particular degree program. Your job, though, is to translate educational abilities into job skills.

You may be lucky by simply stating your grade point average. Again, what does that do for the employer?

Two or four years, or more, of attending college may hold a great deal of meaning. A grade point average may suggest "textbook smarts", but showing how well you interacted with other students and your professors may show your value to an employer. Define your campus extracurricular activities as you would a job.

Acting as liaison between a professor and a community group suggests great interpersonal skills. Acting as an investigative reporter on the school newspaper shows some of the reasoning abilities needed by an employer. Acting as book review editor suggests analytical abilities. Tutoring or making presentations suggests an ability to work closely with people or speak before crowds. Producing a professional portfolio of artwork may get you in the door at an advertising agency. The musical scores you wrote may catch the ear of the producer of television commercials.

Figure out why you are doing the things you're doing. Why do they matter to you? Once you understand the reasoning for your commitments or actions, translate them into job-related benefits. Similarly, listing a few courses you took that may have relevant meaning to an employer is a great way to gain interest and allow for discussion in an interview.

▸ *So you didn't graduate, now what?*

Many times, "life" gets in the way of finishing school. Whether you are into your second semester or one class away from graduation, various things can happen that prevent the continuation of college. If you haven't completed college, do you have to write-off the experience? No, you write it up as a job-related benefit.

Again, what did you get out of the experience. Meeting other students, learning new ideas presented by various professors, or learning to live on your own for the first time—analyze what you got out of the experience. Translate what you have learned as a benefit which would be useful to an employer.

Perhaps an easy way of presenting those qualifications is to list particular classes that support your ability to take on a job. For example, if you were not able to get your degree in accounting, yet have extensive accounting and accounting-related classes, listing those classes may get you the interview from the small company that needs a bookkeeper.

Similarly, the artist that didn't receive her B.F.A. may have a portfolio that outshines all potential competition. Or the writer who never got his B.A. in English, yet has published articles across the country in regional and national publications. The B.A. in English shows the degree; a portfolio of published articles shows the accomplishments. If you never finished high school, have you taken seminars, classes, or company training programs to build your skills? Be ready with a solid reply when you're asked "so, what can you do FOR ME?" Face the facts. Nobody owes you a living. Build your strengths and make the employer realize that they cannot do without you!

▸ *But I've been out of school for ten years!*

Naturally, the more extensive your work experience, the less attention you should pay to detailing educational accomplishments. With a strong work record, simply listing the school, city, state, year graduated and degree granted may be all you need. Still, special accomplishments that fit your particular work interests should be listed if beneficial to your next employer.

For example, awards granted for physics and painting mean different things to different employers. Let's say our job candidate was applying to a paint research facility. In that case, both the physics and painting awards could have meaning to the employer. The employer may appreciate the candidate's technical and scientific abilities, as well as the understanding of the creative applications of paint. Scientifically, a paint may be the best on the market. Aesthetically, it may be the last paint an artist would ever use. An employer wants someone who will make the consumer-oriented judgments necessary to create a great product or service.

Let's review our examples:

Academia

UNIVERSITY OF PHOENIX, Phoenix, AZ
Master of Arts, May 1993
Concentration: Higher Education Administration and Student Development

Bachelor of Arts, January 1990
Major: Political Science

Architect

ILLINOIS INSTITUTE OF TECHNOLOGY, Chicago, IL
A.A.S. Architectural Engineering Technology, May 1989
Major Coursework:

Architectural History and Design	Architectural Design Methods
Architectural Structural Design	Architectural Computer Graphics
Advanced Computer Graphics	Construction Materials Applications
Construction Management	Commercial Building
Mechanical Systems	Estimating, & Specifications

COLUMBIA COLLEGE, Chicago, IL
B.S. in Management Science, 1985
• Dean's List; earned 75% of college expenses.

Architectural Engineer

GEORGIA INSTITUTE OF TECHNOLOGY, Atlanta, GA
B.S. in Architectural Engineering, May 1989

Major Coursework:

Architectural History and Theory	Architectural Design Methods
Construction Management	Commercial Building
Architectural Structural Design	Mechanical Systems
Architectural Computer Graphics	Site Surveying
Advanced Computer Graphics	Physics 1 & 2
Construction Materials Applications	Estimating on Specifications

Art Educator

UNIVERSITY OF SOUTHERN CALIFORNIA, Los Angeles, CA
Bachelor of Arts in Art History, December 1990
Related Coursework:
• Museums & Historical Agencies   • Art Education

- Fundraising for Non-Profit Organizations
- Renaissance Art
- 20th Century Art to 1940
- Art History I & II
- Medieval Art & Religion
- American Painting to 1900

Art History

BOSTON UNIVERSITY, Boston, MA
B.A. in Art History and Italian Studies, May 1988
Coursework: Emphasis on Italian Renaissance Literature and Art
Special Studies: Semester of study in Florence, Italy
                 Semester of study in Venice, Italy

Broadcasting

EMERSON COLLEGE, Boston, MA
Bachelor of Science in Broadcasting and Film, May 1992
G.P.A.: 3.5/4.0
Concentration: Film

Related Coursework:
- Understanding Film
- Film Production I (16 mm)
- Screenwriting
- Art and Craft of the Producer

Business

NATIONAL UNIVERSITY, San Diego, CA
Major in Business Management
Expected graduation in May, 1994
Dean's List; Class Representative

FRENCH INSTITUTE, New York, NY
Certificate in French, Summers 1991/1992

NEW YORK LANGUAGE INSTITUTE, New York, NY
Certificate for English as a second language, 1990

Business Management

AMERICAN UNIVERSITY, Washington, DC
Bachelor of Science in Business Management, May 1993

GEORGETOWN ACADEMY, Washington, DC
College Preparatory Program, May 1989

Business/Operations Management

METROPOLITAN STATE COLLEGE, Denver, CO
Bachelor of Science, *1986*
Major: Business Management

Curriculum Focus:
Salesforce Management; Operations Management; Quantitative Analysis

Micro-computers:
Software including Lotus 1-2-3 and WordPerfect

Chemist

Institution:	Massachusetts Institute of Technology, Cambridge, MA
Degree:	Bachelor of Science, 1989
Major:	Biochemistry
Honors/Awards:	Funded Independent Research Project in Biochemistry
Presentations:	Coronary Artery Bypass Surgery. Presented paper in 1988.
Activities:	Health Aid Volunteer
Sports:	Soccer, football, skiing, tennis.

City Planning

UNIVERSITY OF MINNESOTA, Minneapolis, MN
Master in City Planning, expected 1993
Bachelor of Science, cum laude, 1986

College Activities:
President, Black Student Union
Who's Who in American Colleges and Universities.

Computer Science

WASHINGTON UNIVERSITY, St. Louis, MO
Bachelor of Science degree in Computer Science with an emphasis in Artificial Intelligence, May 1992

ST. LOUIS EDUCATION CENTER, St. Louis, MO
Continuing education studies in Computer Science with an emphasis in Business Data Processing, 1992

Economics

BOSTON UNIVERSITY, Boston, MA
Bachelor of Arts in Economics and Business, May 1992

Relevant Coursework:
Finance, Money and Banking, and Sales Management

Related Information:
- Financed 100% of college tuition
- Worked 30+ hours per week while pursuing degree
- Excellent interpersonal and motivational skills
- Strong time management abilities

Fashion Merchandising

FASHION INSTITUTE OF TECHNOLOGY
Associate of Science, *May 1993*
Major: Fashion Merchandising

Related Coursework:
Fashion Merchandising; Retail Operations; Principles of Color and Line; Textiles; Promotion & Marketing; Fashion Show Production; and various courses in word processing and computer applications.

Finance

QUEENS COLLEGE, Charlotte, NC
B.S.B.A., Concentration in Finance, December, 1992
Honors: Dean's List Fall 1991, Spring 1992
Relevant Coursework: Financial and Managerial Accounting; Management Information Systems; Financial Management; Managerial Economics; Investment Analysis and Portfolio Management; Human Behavior in Organizations; Law and Business; Ethics.
Activities: Reporter for Finance Newsletter; Member, Business Club; Intramural Baseball; Tennis Team.

Interior Designer

COLUMBUS COLLEGE OF ART & DESIGN, Columbus, OH
Bachelor of Science in Interior Design, May 1990
Associates of Science in Interior Design, May 1989
Honors:
National Dean's List; GPA 3.4/4.0

Relevant Skills/Coursework:
Hospitality Design, Commercial Design, Residential Design, Retail and Restaurant Design, Drafting & Rendering, Color & Light, Art History, Foundations of Design, and CADD.

International Law

NEW YORK LAW SCHOOL, New York, NY
LL.M. in International Law, 1988

SUFFOLK UNIVERSITY, Boston, MA
J.D., *Summa Cum Laude*, (Top 3%), 1985
Honor Society, Merit Scholarship,

BOSTON UNIVERSITY, Boston, MA
B.A. in Political Science, *Summa Cum Laude*, 1981
Awarded Outstanding Senior by the Political Science Faculty

International Relations

GEORGETOWN UNIVERSITY, Washington, DC
Bachelor of Arts in International Relations, December 1990
Regional Track: East Asia
Topical Track: International Business and Economics

Related Coursework:
• Contemporary East Asian Economics, International Trade
• International Law and World Order
• International Economics, Money and Banking
• Foreign Policy of the Peoples Republic of China
• Culture and Society of East Asia

Language Instructor

SIMMONS COLLEGE, Boston, MA
Ed.M. Individualized Program: Foreign Language Instruction, 1990

HARVARD UNIVERSITY, Cambridge, MA
B.A. in Chinese Language and Literature, 1986
G.P.A. in Major: 3.7/4.0

HONG KONG LANGUAGE INSTITUTE, Hong Kong
Semester Abroad Program, Advanced level Chinese language and literature studies, 1985

Law - Juris Doctor Candidate

**UNIVERSITY OF CALIFORNIA -
HASTINGS COLLEGE OF LAW**, San Francisco, CA
Candidate for J.D., May 1995
Honorable Mention - First Year Moot Court Section Competition

UNITED STATES INTERNATIONAL UNIVERSITY, San Diego, CA

B.A. in Civic Policy, May 1991
Courses included:
Constitutional Law; Social Psychology; Gender Issues & The Supreme Court; and Prejudice & Discrimination in Rural America.

Honors:
Dean's List, all semesters

Activities:
Resident Assistant in the Office of Residential Services
Publicity Chairperson for Activities Counsel
Volunteer English tutor for other international students

Literature

NORTHEASTERN UNIVERSITY, Boston, MA
Bachelor of Arts, May 1987
Major: English Literature
Minor: Women's Studies

Honors:
Dean's List; Northeastern Scholarship Recipient
Major G.P.A. — 3.7/4.0
Overall G.P.A. — 3.3/4.0

Merchandising

MARIAN COLLEGE, Indianapolis, IN
Bachelor of Science in Merchandising; Minor in Business Administration, 1988
Academic Scholarship Recipient

Music Production & Engineering

UNIVERSITY OF SOUTHERN CALIFORNIA, Los Angeles, CA
Bachelor of Music Degree in Music Production and Engineering, *1993*
Bachelor of Music Degree in Music Synthesis, *1993*
Coursework: 24 track Engineering; 24 track Mixdown; Masters Engineering; Hard disk recording; Live sound; Sound design.

Physician

Institution: University of Medicine and Dentistry of New Jersey, Newark, NJ
Degree: Doctor of Medicine, May 1991
Honors/Awards: Health Scholarship
Organizations: AMSA, AMA, New Jersey Medical Society
Activities: Squash, tennis, rowing, volleyball, and skiing

Publishing

CASE WESTERN RESERVE UNIVERSITY, Cleveland, OH
Master of Arts — Writing, Literature and Publishing, May 1991

CLEVELAND STATE UNIVERSITY, Cleveland, OH
Bachelor of Science Degree, *summa cum laude, May 1989*
Major: Advertising
G.P.A. 3.8/4.0

Relevant Coursework:

Graphic Arts   Newspaper Journalism
Newswriting   Copywriting
Photography   Advertising

Social Worker

NEW YORK UNIVERSITY, New York, NY
Master of Arts in Social Sciences, *1983*

YESHIVA UNIVERSITY, New York, NY
Bachelor of Arts in Social Sciences, *1978*
Concentration in Sociology and Psychology

Other Studies:

NEW YORK UNIVERSITY, New York, NY
18 credit hours toward a Masters of Social Work, *1990 - Present*

NEW YORK ADVOCACY GROUP, New York, NY
Seminars in Alcohol Counseling, Supervising At-Risk Adolescents, and Resolving
Conflicts in School Settings, *1987 - 1990*

Presenting your education on your résumé is fairly straightforward. As you should note from the examples, though, you may be able to amplify this category by more specifically highlighting the things you participated in as relevant to a future employer.

Now, move on to "The Extras." Do not discount all the wonderful other things you have done that will show how valuable you will become to your next employer.

THE EXTRAS

▼
AKA's:

Awards	*Special Skills*	*Languages*
Interests	*Honors*	*Internships*
Seminars	*Civic Interests*	*Community Service*
Affiliations	*System Skills*	*Memberships*
Activities	*Technical Skills*	*Volunteer Work*
Other Data	*Programming Skills*	*Research Projects*
Computer Languages	*Hardware Knowledge*	*Software Knowledge*
Extracurricular Activities	*Special Projects*	*Workshops*
Community Involvement	*Corporate Affiliations*	*Travel*
Publications	*Works-in-Progress*	*Presentation Skills*
Coaching Skills	*Leadership Abilities*	

You have other skills that may benefit your job search and your résumé. You have to determine whether or not to include these "extras" based on how helpful they'll be to your presentation. Do not consider these categories to be superfluous, "filler" material. Many of these categories are vitally important to some employers. Depending on the nature of activity or interest, you may find one or more of these categories to be a determining factor in getting the job.

Let's review some of these categories. We'll review them in terms of why you might want to include them on your résumé.

▶ *Community Activities*

There are activities you may take part of in your community which may show leadership, your ability to be a team player, your knowledge of a certain subject matter or region of your town, etc. For example, if you were a Choral Director at your local church, with responsibility for collecting funds, making purchases, and setting up travel itineraries for regional performances, you could certainly write about proven skills and abilities in that context. Ability to manage groups of people, trustworthiness with funds, interpersonal skills — if you contribute to any community activities, decide if your participation and applicable skills would help a future employer. If so, write up your strengths.

▶ *Computer Skills*

Whether your specialty is programming, data entry, using graphic software applications, or some other computer design, processing, or technical ability, you should certainly give special attention to your abilities on the résumé. As more companies streamline their operations, managers are having to rely on less administrative assistance and support staff are being required to have much broader skills.

The manager or support person who can create a spreadsheet using Lotus 1-2-3, generate reports with innovative pie charts, incorporate graphics into a client brochure using the Macintosh, etc., will be much in demand as the company competes with aggressive competitors.

Remember to always volunteer for as much training as possible in computer technologies. Single, specific skills may become obsolete. Become multi-talented and always be relied on in the office as a valuable resource. If three Vice Presidents rely on you to get reports to their clients on time, do you think you have value? And if you are asked to learn new computer applications to get the work done faster and with a more elegant look for those same clients, do you think a VP won't appreciate your efforts and talent? (If not — boy, will you be marketable elsewhere!)

As your company changes its focus, combines divisions, rewrites job descriptions — demands more and more from each employee — always have the skills necessary to compete with the best the company has to offer.

▶ Affiliations

Listing various organizations that you belong to or contribute to suggests personality traits to the reader. If you belong to an historical association, a county board overseeing relations with local police, etc., you will intrigue or possibly alienate the résumé reader. However you present your affiliations, feel comfortable discussing related subjects in the interview and possibly defending your interests.

For example, listing your affiliation with the Young Republicans of New Hampshire, you may interview with a staunch Republican who wants to talk about whipping some Democrat's butt. Or, your résumé may be discarded (or worse) by a very liberal Democrat who couldn't bear to have you as a direct report, let alone shake your hand in an interview.

You have every right to list affiliations that are important to you. Just be sure that any adverse reaction is acceptable to you, that a company upset with your affiliations may not be a place for you to work anyway. If the company promotes "on the books" or discreet discrimination that affects you personally (remember some of those major examples of discrimination shown in the press in the early 1990s?), it's probably best that you not begin a working partnership with them at all. Work affects the soul; don't corrupt your ideals.

▶ The Extras You Don't Need

Some things, for the most part, do not need to be on your résumé. In most instances, a category does not need to be on the résumé called "PERSONAL." Your sex, health, marital status, weight, height, or age do not normally need to be on your résumé. None of these things is a skill.

With that said, a few fields do require some things most other employers wouldn't need for their evaluation process. For example, a cruise line may want a recent photograph of you attached to the upper corner of the résumé. Perhaps they'll also want to know if you are a great dancer. Specifically, what steps have you mastered? Though nobody can force you to put something on your résumé, the hotel chain may like the fact that you have listed "single; willing to relocate" at the bottom of the résumé.

A great résumé has many defined qualities. Still, some "extras" totally depend on the job, the employer, your personality, and more. As long as you accept everything you have put on your résumé and don't mind the employer's reaction, positive or negative, you'll be confident that you have done the right thing.

Here are many categories for you to consider:

Academic Awards

- *Physics Prize — maintained highest competitive position out of 65 students.*
- *Academic Award*
- *Italian Language—Honorable Mention*
- *Mathematics—Honorable Mention*

Academic Honors

- International Law Journal, Case and Note Editor
- Awarded Certificate of Excellence for Highest Grade in Federal Courts by the Federal Bar Association, Arkansas Chapter
- Winner, American Jurisprudence Prize Award: Highest Grade in Family Law
- Named Spiegelmann Scholar — GPA within top 10% of first-year section

Accounting Memberships

Member, American Institute of Certified Public Accountants; Tax Division and Partnership Taxation Committee
Member, Society of Certified Public Accountants; Real Estate Committee

Activities

Entrepreneur's Association(Member); Minorities in Management(Active Member); Big Brother Association(Big Brother)

Affiliations

American Institute of Chemical Engineers
Air and Waste Management Association

Affiliations

Member, National Association of Social Workers (NASW)
Member, American Society on Aging (ASA)

Art Shows

Shaner Gallery, New York, NY

Show of large-scale works done in oil.
Published drawings for 2 newspapers — SoHo News and The Journal, in connection with exhibit traveling to the Rose Art Museum in Massachusetts.

Banking Seminars

- Received Certificate of National Banking from the American Banking Institute
- Completed and passed the first year of the Mortgage Bankers Association of America, School of Mortgage Banking
- Completed seminars on Professional Selling Skills, Business Writing, and the Executive Challenge Program

Business Management Seminars

The Legal Aspects of Purchasing
Dealing with Vendors & Suppliers
The Supervisor as a Member of Management
Basic Supervision

Business Skills

- Lotus 1-2-3
- WordPerfect 5.0
- Microsoft Works
- Bookkeeping
- Payroll
- Typing
- Excellent Writing and Communication Skills

Business Skills

- Keyboard Speed: 40+ w.p.m.
- IBM PCs — Novell networked
- IBM Selectric typewriters
- Wang — Minicomputers and PCs

College Activities

BOSTON UNIVERSITY ALUMNI ASSOCIATION
As Community Service Chairman, organized and coordinated community events.

SIGMA CHI EPSILON NATIONAL FRATERNITY
Inter-Fraternity/Sorority Delegate

College Activities

- American Planning Association — Student Regional Representative
- Senator, Graduate School Representative
- International Student Government

College Interests/Activities

- Sports, particularly running and aerobic exercises.
- Membership in Public Relations Student Society of America.
- Extensive travel throughout the United States, Europe, and the Middle East.
- Advanced independent product research in exercise equipment and health marketing strategies.

Computer/Programming Skills

Software:
Matlab, Micro-Cap III, MS Windows, PC-DSP, Mathmatica, MathCAD, Schema III+, Workview, Lotus 1-2-3.

Languages:
"C", Turbo Pascal, Assembler.

Hardware:
IBM PC, Macintosh, VAX 6000-420, ADSP-2101, Tektronix Fourier Analyzer.

Computer/Programming Skills

Hardware
- IBM 3090, IBM PC XT, IBM 4381, IBM 3083, VAX 8600, VAX 780, and Honeywell 66/DPS3

Languages
- COBOL, SAS, CSP, RPG, PL/1

Software
- DB2/SQL, IMS/DLI, CICS, OS/JCL, VSAM, MVS/XA, DOS, TSO/ISPF, LOTUS

Computing Skills

Higher Programming Languages: BASIC, PASCAL, FORTRAN, and C; *Assembler:* Z80, M68000 Microprocessor Systems; *Word Processing:* Lotus Manuscript/Word; *Data Processing:* Lotus 1-2-3.

Editorial Credentials

- Edited articles and worked with authors to develop pieces; Conducted research and wrote pertinent articles.

Articles, Papers, Presentations:

- Empowerment in School-Based Management
- Action Learning and Organizational Development
- Managing Total Quality Performance
- Cooperative Education

Other projects:
- Numerous classified studies, reports, and presentations.
- On-going research: managing diversity; conflict and change; curriculum improvement in a multicultural environment.

Education Affiliations

CEA — Cooperative Education Association
NEACEFE — New England Association for Cooperative Education and Field Experience

Food Service Certification

NATIONAL INSTITUTE FOR THE FOOD SERVICE INDUSTRY (NIFI)
Sanitation Certificate; Awarded for demonstrating knowledge of proper preparation, handling, and serving of food.

Geographical Preferences

Geographical Preference - Miami area.
No business travel constraints.

Hardware Knowledge

IBM Mainframe System (36, 38, 3031, 4381), IBM PC and Clones, TRS-80, Four-phase system, VAX system, Sperry-80, Apple PC, Macintosh, Magnetic Tape, Disk Drives, Micro Fiche Recorder and Developer, Line and Character Printers, and Telecommunication hardware.

Health Services Affiliations

- National Health Promotion Network
- American Psychological Association
- American Public Health Association
- Public Health Association

High School Honors

Who's Who of American High School Students
Recipient of The Juliard School's Achievement Award for music performance and composition.

Insurance Licenses

- Chartered Property and Casualty Underwriter (C.P.C.U.), 1978
- Fully licensed Insurance Broker in California
- Licensed Insurance Advisor in California

Languages

- French, German, Spanish, and Russian (with varying degrees of fluency).
- Italian and Polish (reading with varying degrees of fluency; translated letters from Italian to English as part of graduate program).
- Japanese (current enrollment in intensive language study program).

Languages

- Fluent in French, German, Spanish, and English.
- Intensive German studies in Lindau, Germany.
- Intensive German studies in Bregenz, Austria.
- Intensive English studies at CEEL, Geneva.

Licenses

- Securities and Exchange Commission; Series 7
- Uniform Securities State Commission; Series 63
- Northeast Region Life Insurance License

License/Certification

Licensed Certified Social Worker
Commonwealth of Massachusetts
Board of Registration
#1056 5 03819

Medical Training

- *Assertive Management*
- *Stress Reduction*
- *Time Management*
- *Hospital Supervision*
- *AIDS Awareness*
- *Nutrition*
- *Anorexia and Bulemia*
- *Counseling Skills Development*

Medical Training

- Trained as an Emergency Medical Technician (EMT)

• American Heart Association CPR Instructor

Military Honors

• *Good Conduct Medal*
• *Army Achievement Medal*
• *Army Accommodation Medal*
• *Air Assault Badge*

Military Honors

Army ROTC: Sergeant
Best Efforts Academically
Student Leadership Participation
First Aide Certification
CPR Certification
Safety Committee

Military Honors

• Combat Action and National Defense
• Prisoner Escort Qualified
• Demolitions Expert
• Good Conduct Medal
• Rifle and Pistol Expert, 4th Award Badges
• Platoon Letter of Appreciation

Military Training

Primary Marksmanship Instructor School
Rifle/Pistol Certificate

Prisoner Escort School
Certificate

School Of Infantry
Certificate

Music Achievements

Diploma in Performance — Violin
Winner of Young Musician Competitions
Conductor of College Chamber Choir
Author of musical compositions
Voted "Most Likely to Succeed" in Class of '92

Music Honors

High School Music Awards included:
Award for Outstanding Musicianship
High School National Championship - Violin
High School State Festival Award — Best Ensemble Performance
Central District Orchestra Championships — Finalist

Musical/Technical Abilities

- Advanced music reading and writing skills used in music recording, recording techniques and procedures.
- Sound recording training on professional equipment, using different recording techniques for various types of music.
- Experience as a second recording engineer.
- Working with MIDI, automated mixing and micing.

Office Skills

Advanced Typing (70+ wpm)
Word Processing - WordPerfect 5.1
Legal Office Procedures
Lotus 1-2-3
Legal Machine Transcription
Advanced Shorthand (110+ wpm)
Legal Dictation and Transcription
Effective Writing for Business

Personal Data

- Age 25
- Single, willing to relocate, nationally or internationally
- U.S. Citizen
- Excellent Health

Professional Affiliations

Member: Massachusetts Association of College Admissions Counselors
Board Member and Volunteer: Immigrant Tutoring Program

Professional Memberships

- Strategic-Consultant Group — Strategic Planning — Industrial Development in Mexico
- South American Planning Association
- Urban Land Institute

- International Personnel Management Association
- South American Society of Public Administration
- Community Development Society

Real Estate Credentials

Real Estate Finance Association
Houston Real Estate Board
- ***Chairman*** — Certificate in Real Estate Finance Committee Program
- ***Course Instructor*** — Commercial Loan Workouts

Sales Training

- Charles Givens Sales and Negotiation Seminar
- Corporate Dynamics "Selling with Impact!" Seminar
- Brian Tracy's "Psychology of Selling" Program
- Napoleon Hill's "Mastering the Keys to Success" Program

Sales Training

Tom Hopkins Competitive Edge Selling (1993)
Brian Tracy Selling Seminar (1992)
Active participant in over 15 in-house training programs sponsored by AT&T

Scholarships

INTERNATIONAL PROGRAMS OFFICE SCHOLARSHIP
Awarded an educational scholarship by the International Programs Office, University of Texas

Software Abilities

BASIC, ANS COBOL, Structured COBOL, CICS, Pascal, ORACLE, SQL, DBASE III, "C", JCL/OCL, Operating Systems (MS-DOS), an assortment of word processors, spreadsheets, and telecommunication software.

Special Projects

- Developed new product marketing and advertising campaign proposals, including ad concept, creation of storyboards, forecasting, preplanning, and preparation of ad campaign budgets.
- Analyzed income statements and overall financial status, developed methods to improve sales, marketing, and management strategies.
- Conducted research and developed plans to increase enrollment in voluntary corporate training program.

Sports Activities & Awards

- Study of Tai-Chi for 7 years and currently
- Private Instructor in Tai-Chi
- Member of Boy Scouts of America — Star Scout; member of Order of the Arrow

Sports & Community Activities

BOSTON YOUTH TENNIS PROGRAM, Roxbury, MA
Serving as Captain and Treasurer

BOY SCOUTS AND CAMPFIRE GIRLS OF AMERICA, Boston, CA
Class Leader and Tutor

System Skills

- Computer programming in Pascal, BASIC, COBOL, and Assembler.
- Excellent technical knowledge of Lotus 1-2-3, WordPerfect, and Word.
- Knowledge of MS-DOS based computers as well as Macintosh, Atari, and Amiga.

Teaching Skills

- Experienced in E.S.L. (English/Spanish).
- Transitional Instruction (Four Years).
- Instructed students with varying academic skills.
- Implemented individualized instructional techniques for special needs participants.
- Coordinated the Learning and Emotionally Disadvantaged program run by area social service agencies.

Technical/Computer Skills
Technical
- Drafting on mylar with plastic lead and technical pens
- Renderings
- Production of commercial working drawings

Computer
- DataCad in 2D and 3D graphics
- Construction software — Timberline, Supercalc, Harvard project planner
- WordPerfect

Technical Skills

- 8mm & 16mm film format
- 1/2 & 3/4 inch video format
- Macintosh graphics software
- Sony U-Matic editing machines

Travel

France (travel and residence), Canada, Germany, Switzerland, Austria, Netherlands, Italy, Denmark, Great Britain, Spain, and throughout the United States.

Travel Seminars

Retail Travel — Use of manuals in retail travel industry for foreign and domestic travel, with emphasis on air, land, and sea transportation.

Comprehensive Travel Planning — Procedures for packaging worldwide independent and group travel.

Introduction to Travel Industry Computer Systems — Principles and capabilities of computers.

Travel Management and Planning — Emphasis on group travel, corporate travel, tour operating, and convention planning.

Volunteer Work

Volunteer to help with brain-injured children in senior year of college; Member of Student Government and Yearbook Committee

Writing Awards

- *Founder of an independent poetry magazine, now in its third year of publication.*
- *Member of Summer Arts Program — creative writing workshop.*
- *Scholarship Recipient — $3,000 — "For Outstanding Leadership Potential"*

Whatever your "extras" may be — technical skills, computer skills, travel experience, language abilities, etc. — give weight to those things that the employer will find useful, impressive, or worth talking about in an interview.

▶ Final Tip

Don't forget all the valuable contacts you have made gaining these added skill sets and participating in various activities. Recognize that someone is teaching you a skill and offers expertise in his or her subject matter. This person probably belongs to related associations, subscribes to useful magazines and journals, has contacts throughout an industry, etc. Remember that much of your research and assistance can be obtained by just asking! Ask, ask, ask!!

Most people are willing to lend a supportive hand if asked to do so. This chapter should have identified many categories that might apply to your life history. If appropriate, use them on your résumé. Most importantly, ask the people related to these "extras" to help you succeed in your job search campaign.

LAYOUT, TYPEFACES, PAPERS, ETC.

Once all of your writing and revisions have been completed, you have to consider best methods for presentation. We do not recommend that you pull out the old typewriter (you know, the one with the jammed 'M' key) and type the document.

Great care should go into the preparation of your résumé. In my other book, <u>The Smart Job Search—A Guide to Proven Methods for Finding a Great Job</u>, we talked about the value of a customer. Briefly, we stated that a person has value to a company based over the whole term they'll shop with that company. Thus, spending $100 a week at a grocery store for 5 years actually means your value to that store is at least $26,000! Shouldn't you be treated with respect for that kind of money? (The next time you receive bad or rude service, remind the manager what is at stake!)

Similarly, if you are looking to spend 4 or 5 years at a job that pays $25,000 per year, you should realize that the company will be paying you over $100,000 or more (plus any benefits). Shouldn't you go out of your way to take great care in your presentation for that kind of money? If you received one fat check for $125,000, wouldn't you expect to have accomplished something pretty substantial to get that much money?

You've now created a great résumé presenting many strengths and accomplishments. With so much care in the creation, don't lose out of career opportunities due to lack of a great presentation.

Also, remember that none of us lives in a solitary world. The way you present yourself now may have an impact on a whole host of future events. An example will explain.

Assume you've applied for a job you are not qualified for. You know your chances of getting the job are practically zero. You'd like to work for the company but you've not seen any appropriate openings. With these factors in mind, should you give half-hearted effort to your presentation? Absolutely not!

Why? First, a professional-looking résumé suggests that you respect yourself. Second, in almost all companies, people know other people. Friendships are formed throughout and across multiple divisions. Your résumé may travel throughout several divisions and end up precisely in the department where you want to work. Third and finally, companies are desperate for qualified workers. A person who'll contribute wonderful things will be brought to the attention of many people. You've heard the story of the person who travels halfway around the world only to unexpectedly meet their next door neighbor? You'll never know for sure who knows about you or cares about you. Don't cut off any possible opportunities.

This long preamble to our discussion on layouts, typefaces, papers, etc. has been written simply to highlight how very important résumés are to a successful career path.

▶ *Your Presentation*

I suggest you <u>not</u> use binders or "presentation packets/pockets" offered by some professional services. A one-page résumé, printed on fine quality, 24 lb. paper should be acceptable. Further, don't attach a photograph or cover page announcing the document — "Private and Confidential: The

Résumé of Janice Jones" — packages such as these just look too contrived, plus they waste valuable time, keeping attention away from your strengths and abilities.

▸ *Page Layout*

Certainly try to keep your résumé to one page only. I believe if you offer less than eight to fourteen years of professional experience you must stay to one page. For best visual effect, leave a top margin of 1/2", bottom margin of 1/2 to 3/4", left margin of 3/4", and right margin of 1". This small amount of extra space on the right margin is suggested due to the empty space created by the categories column — "experience, " "education," and so on.

Study the examples in the "Sample Résumés" chapter. You will see that visual elegance is achieved using this method.

▸ *Typefaces*

The typeface is simply the way the letters and words look on the page. There are literally thousands of typefaces that can be used, with more being created every year!

Most computers offer a few standard typefaces to choose from. For each example in the "Sample Résumés" chapter, I have not only listed the professions but the typeface used as well. Also, for most examples, a 10 point typeface was used. Many computers use a default setting of 12 points; you should change to 10 points to arrive at the cleanest, most professional look. If changing the typeface leaves you too much space at the bottom of your document, consider adding a bit of extra space between categories. A type size that is too large looks as if you were writing a high school or college term paper. Graduate to the real world and use a 10 point typeface.

▸ *Paper*

As said before, a 24 lb. stock is acceptable. Paper color should be determined by your profession. For the most part, an ivory, white, or grey paper are the most preferred choices. If you are not confident about which papers may be right for you, stay with one of these and you will be all right.

At Smart Résumés in Boston, I work with area colleges that represent all types of fields and areas of expertise. Boston University's School of Management, Berklee College of Music, Emerson College, Boston Architectural Center, and literally dozens of other area colleges and universities prepare our future experts, from international relations, accounting, and communications to music production, acting, and architecture professionals. And hundreds more!

For this audience, my company offers nine different paper choices. They are all elegant, yet some are very different than a plain ivory or white. Select paper according to your career field.

▸ *Your Audience*

Be as different as you like with your paper choice and the design of your document. Just remember to make sure the paper and look fit your profession. What an actress can do is much different than what is appropriate for a banker. Every job demands professionalism in its own context.

▶ *Where to go? Where to go?*

Should you do the résumé yourself? Should you take it to a copy center? Should you go to a counselor? A résumé specialist? There are many options. They have their own risks and rewards.

My company, Smart Résumés, in Boston, rarely advertises because our referrals are very high. I am proud that we are rewarded for quality service and a great product. Likewise, in your community you should ask around (to those who will maintain your confidentiality, of course). Employment agencies, career resource centers at local colleges, family and friends, and many others can suggest who is great or not so wonderful. If you prefer, we would welcome serving you — just refer to the information provided in the "Conclusion" chapter.

Asking detailed questions of at least a few résumé services is very important. Never choose to have a résumé done without comparing all services and prices various firms offer. If you ask around and know what to ask, you'll find quality and service at a price you can afford.

We tell our Smart Résumés clients to compare us against our competition by asking about the following:

1. *Expertise.* Does the service offer expertise in the field? Besides my books, I offer seminars and workshops for various groups on how to write a résumé, as well as speak to listeners via radio talk shows and write articles on aspects of the job search process. Making use of a copy center or friend offering a computer and printer is not your best strategy when years of future employment are affected by that one piece of paper.

2. *Assistance.* Is the company pleasant to deal with and does it readily offer suggestions and help, without charging you for every "quick tip?"

3. *Price.* Does a price list exist for you to take home. You should not have to worry about being "priced" according to your look of affluence, or desperation. Beware the intangible "package" that offers vague promises (e.g., a free rewrite of your résumé if you follow strict rules over a 6-week period in your job search. If the résumé is written correctly in the first place, why would you need it rewritten? And why should you pay dearly for such a vague promise?) You need to know, in detail, what prices are for every service offered.

4. *A Full Service.* Can the company help you with all the things you'll need to do. You will be writing your résumé, cover letters, a reference list, follow-up letters, and more. You should be able to rely on one company to provide all of these services at a reasonable cost.

5. *Speed.* You cannot afford to drop your material off to a company and wait two or three, or more, weeks to receive your first proof back from the service. My company's normal time for turnaround is one business day. The longest period we need to turnaround a résumé is three business days — and that is if we do all of the writing! Being in Boston, with a huge college population, Smart Résumés thrives because we are experts, do a superb job, and complete assignments quickly for a vast array of professionals and future professionals.

6. *Permanent Storage.* Now, with computers, you should not have to begin the résumé process over from scratch each time you begin looking for a job. Also, if you use a professional service,

you should feel they want your business and will do editing and reprinting services at a reasonable cost.

7. *Postscript Laser Printing.* All of your documents should be laser printed. Beware the company offering laser printing where in reality the first print is a laser and the rest are just photocopies. Everything done for you should be laser printed.

8. *Confidentiality.* Many people look for jobs while employed. A résumé service should respect your need for privacy. Do you feel the copy center that does résumés as a sideline will offer confidentiality and professionalism needed in this tough job market? Also, do you want someone to do your résumé who is just doing the work while searching for their own future career, perhaps in the same field as your own?

9. *Guarantee.* How happy must you be with the résumé service? At Smart Résumés, we take no "advance," "retainer," or "deposit." We ask for payment, in full, when a client picks up their résumé. They have every right to refuse the work we've done for them if they are not satisfied — with us, that just doesn't happen.

Being in the résumé business, I realize how crucially important a great résumé is to your future success. Consider carefully how you will prepare your résumé. For example, I know how to do my own laundry, iron my clothing, and buy all associated materials to get the job done. Could I, therefore, walk into a dry cleaning company and take over all operations? Of course not. Similarly, if you know how to type, set a margin, and have the ability to list your work history, don't assume you are guaranteed a great résumé. I have created thousands of documents for people. Still, my 6050th document is better than my 5th. This book is giving you years of my expertise, but if you need more, get professional help.

Approximately 60% of my firm's business comes via referrals. I know we create a great product and deliver what we promise to do. My business is very important to me. Your résumé should be vitally important to you.

Résumé Examples by Profession

PETER STANFORD

Current Address:
Box 816 - B5A, OCU
Oklahoma City, OK 73106

Permanent Address:
12 Ware Street
Bethany, OK 73008
(405) 495 - 1196

PROFESSIONAL GOAL

To utilize strong academic knowledge and internship experience and contribute to an entry level position in a public accounting firm.

EDUCATION

OKLAHOMA CITY UNIVERSITY, Oklahoma City, OK
Bachelor of Science Degree, May 1993
Concentration in Accounting
Minor in Economics
GPA: 3.91/4.0
Concentration GPA: 3.94/4.0

Relevant Coursework:

- Law for Accountants
- International Accounting
- Non-Profit Organizations and the IRS
- Advanced Taxation
- Corporate Taxation
- Financial Institution Management
- Management Information Systems
- International Relations

COMPUTER SKILLS

Lotus 1-2-3, BASIC, dBase III+, WordPerfect 5.1, and general knowledge of various accounting software applications.

INTERNSHIP EXPERIENCE

FOUNDERS BANK & TRUST COMPANY, Oklahoma City, OK   Summers 1992 & 1993
Administrative Assistant
- Assisted an account officer with institutional accounts valued at over $3 billion.
- Handle transactions and resolved out-of-balance account problems for a wide range of accounts including correspondent banks, schools, and foundations.

Daily duties included:
- Purchasing and selling repurchase agreements.
- Maintaining cash positions and moving funds to maintain positive balances in accounts.
- Preparing weekly reports for account officer's review.
- Handling correspondence with clients and their advisors.

Monthly duties:
- Calculating interest accruals and amortizations on certain portfolios and their investments, generating reports to be sent to clients.
- Verifying that all accounts (over 100) were properly charged by fee unit.

OTHER EXPERIENCE

STANFORD CLEANING, Bethany, OK   Summers 1987 - 1990
Partner
- Set up business to perform indoor and outdoor house cleaning and repair service.
- Built client list to over 50 weekly and monthly accounts, with responsibilities for general yard work, painting houses and fences, indoor painting, cleaning out drains, and many other various duties.
- Sold business to other partner for $3,500 and maintain 6% share of gross receipts.

TECHNICAL SKILLS

CERTIFICATE IN CARPENTRY
Awarded certificate in construction procedures for wood frame and commercial buildings.
- Extensive coursework in estimating and scheduling for project development.

LANGUAGES

General understanding of Spanish.

REFERENCES

References and letters of recommendation available upon request.

MARK JOHNSTON
1865 North First Street, #320
San Jose, CA 95131
(408) 441 - 0942

OBJECTIVE   To build upon a strong academic record and professional experience to obtain an accounting position.

EDUCATION   **LOYOLA MARYMOUNT UNIVERSITY**, Los Angeles, CA
Bachelor of Science in Accounting, magna cum laude, December 1989
GPA in Major: 3.8/4.00

Relevant Coursework:
□ Financial Accounting I & II
□ Labor Economics
□ Principles of Money and Economics
□ International Economics
□ Environmental Law & Business

Activities:
□ Varsity Soccer
□ Editor of "The Ledger," the college's economic newsletter.

PROFESSIONAL EXPERIENCE   **SAN JOSE ECONOMIC RESEARCH GROUP**, San Jose, CA   1990 - Present
Financial Analyst
• Research portfolios and provide account managers with analysis to make investment decisions.
• Maintain daily contact with clients with over $10 million in equity or liquid portfolios.
• Promoted to supervisory position within three months of hire date.

WELLS FARGO BANK, San Francisco, CA   Summer 1988
Research Assistant
• Performed research for financial analysts, with particular emphasis on global currencies.
• Participated in trade settlements and resolving account discrepancies.

OTHER EXPERIENCE   **WORLD LIMOUSINE SERVICE**, San Jose, CA   Summer 1989
Supervisor
• Oversaw and dispatched drivers throughout San Jose and surrounding areas.
• Trained new employees and supervised proper handling and maintenance of vehicles.

OUTWARD BOUND, Camden, ME   Summers 1986 - 1987
Volunteer
• Participated in program which teaches team commitment and survival in harsh environmental conditions.
• Developed strong communication, organizational, and leadership skills.

LANGUAGES   Verbal and written proficiency in Spanish and Italian.

INTERESTS   Hiking, biking, racquetball, and guitar.

REFERENCES   Available upon request.

Profession: Accountant/Researcher   Typeface: Adobe Garamond

FRED PERRY
9189 Montgomery Road
Cincinnati, OH 45242
(513) 791 - 7826

Age: 27   Height: 5' 11"   Weight: 165

Hair: Light Brown   Eyes: Dark Blue

FILM EXPERIENCE

Role	*Film*	*Location*
Antony	Julius Caesar	Emerson College
Shannon	Night of the Iguana	Emerson College

STAGE EXPERIENCE

Role	*Play*	*Location*
He	Snackers	Portland, ME
Shannon	Night of the Iguana	Portland, ME
Sampson	Romeo and Juliet	Portsmouth, NH
Trespasser	The Field	Boston, MA
Romeo	Romeo and Juliet	Boston, MA
Babes in Arms	Extra	Boston, MA

EDUCATION

Emerson College, Boston, MA
Bachelor of Arts, *cum laude*, 1992
Emphasis on Voice and Communication

HONORS

Awarded Boston Community Award for service to inner city youth
programs, 1991

Drama Prize, 1990

SKILLS

Playwriting; Improvisation; Competitive Swimming; Archery

LANGUAGES

General reading and speaking ability in Spanish.

Profession: Actor   Typeface: Helvetica

Profession: Actress   Typeface: Avant Garde Book Oblique

MELINDA HAWTHORNE
198 Bellevue Avenue • Newport, RI 02840
(401) 849 - 5581

Height: 5' 9"   Weight: 130
Eyes: Blue   Hair: Auburn
Age Range: 18 - 30   Singing Range: Soprano
Character Types: Wide Range

PRODUCTION:	CHARACTER:	THEATER/LOCATION:
The Club	Bobby	Avery Theater, Cleveland, OH
Picnic	Irma Kronkite	Avery Theater, Cleveland, OH
My Fair Lady	Eliza Doolittle	Community Troupe, Newport, RI
A Chorus Line	Chorus	Majic Theater, Dayton, OH
West Side Story	Graziella	Davies Stage, Providence, RI
Funny Girl	Chorus	Showman Stage, Cleveland, OH
Our Town	Emily Webb	Kennedy's, Dallas, TX
Sweet Charity	Rosie	Community Troupe, Newport, RI
Into the Woods	Rapunzel	Community Troupe, Newport, RI

COMMERCIALS:

Passerby in Diet Coke 30-second spot.
Bicyclist in Avia 30-second spot.
Crowd Participant in Pepsi 30-second spot.

INDUSTRIAL SHOWS:

Dancer for the Cleveland Auto Show.
Singer for the Midwest Computer Software Show.
Model for the Newport Tourism and Commerce Show.

TV VOICEOVERS:

Wife for Mel's World Discounters, a one-minute spot.

MODELING:

Runway model for Dayton Spring Fashion Show.

PROFESSIONAL TRAINING:

Nico Samara	Voice	Boston, MA
Prunella Dixon	Voice	Boston, MA
Margert Johnson	Jazz	Dayton, OH
Kevin Horton	Acting	New York, NY
Dance Ensemble	Tap; Ballet	New York, NY

SPECIAL SKILLS

Cheerleading, Dancing, Roller Skating, Bicycling, Tap, Ballet, Aerobics, Southern Dialects, Modeling, Sign Language, and Video Performance Art.

PORTFOLIO

Extensive print and video portfolio available upon request.

JOYCE HAVILAND
218 South Prospect Avenue
Park Ridge, IL 60068
(312) 823 - 7671

GOAL

To obtain an administrative support position which will utilize strong computer, administrative, and interpersonal skills.

SUMMARIZED BY

- Over 5 years in client services with proven ability to work with all levels of staff and management.
- Excellent skills handling clients and resolving their concerns.
- Solid experience using WordPerfect 5.1, Microsoft Word 5.0, PageMaker, and MacDraw.
- Analytical strength, successfully working through problems and implementing solutions.
- Effective team participation needed to realize company goals.

WORK EXPERIENCE

QUALITY ASSURANCE FOCUS GROUP, Park Ridge, IL   1990 - Present
Administrative Assistant

- Maintained correspondence and contact with academic groups, government agencies, and domestic and international banks.
- Updated account information using WordPerfect 5.1.
- Received and processed orders on a daily basis and provided senior managers with weekly tracking reports of activity.
- Solved client complaints via written and telephone communications.
- Organized research data and created reports for supervisor's review.
- Updated sales lead lists and provided sales team with weekly prospecting reports.
- Handled training for new co-op students.

COLLEGE DATA GROUP, Chicago, IL   1988 - 1990
Promotions Assistant

- Prepared newsletter using Macintosh computers, Microsoft Word, and MacDraw software.
- Helped write press releases for on-air use and in corporate correspondence.
- Researched and compiled information for use in developing direct mail campaigns to area colleges and businesses.

MIDWEST SECURITIES TRUST COMPANY, Chicago, IL   1985 - 1988
Secretary

- Scheduled and organized conferences, meetings, and client functions.
- Set up video teleconferencing network affecting 200 staff and 3 offices in different states.
- Handled all correspondence for Vice President, with responsibility for setting up daily schedules.

EDUCATION

ROOSEVELT UNIVERSITY
Undergraduate studies in Liberal Arts, 1984 - 1985

**MIDWEST SECURITIES TRUST/
CHICAGO STATE UNIVERSITY COLLABORATIVE**
Certificate in Data Processing, Fall 1985

THE DRAKE TRAINING PROGRAM
Certificate in Function Planning, Summer 1990

REFERENCES

Available upon request.

Profession: Administrative Assitant   Typeface: Helvetica

BLAINE KOPP
361 First Avenue South
Seattle, WA
(206) 622 - 3376

SUMMARY	❑ Over 11 years of proven management support positions with medium sized growth companies.
	❑ Performing to the highest level of customer service, resolving client problems and retaining solid client base.
	❑ Preparing detailed reports for management to plan strategies for future growth.

AREAS OF EXPERTISE

Operations
- Manage the daily activities of nine staff members, with overall reporting responsibilities to 20 officers.
- Prepare senior level reports which outline monthly performance results for each officer, broken down by new contacts, sales to new and existing clients, and profit ratios by product line.
- Supervise three staff handling client problems; resolve account issues, process trades, and create specialized reports.

Training
- Deliver monthly training seminars throughout the corporation; plan, budget, and set schedules for 5 divisions covering over 200 employees.
- Write project plans and training manuals for classes taught by 2 trainers.
- Implement "train the trainer" programs teaching one individual from each division to ensure continuous skills development.

Purchasing
- Oversee $200,000+ operating budget for all supplies used throughout corporate headquarters.
- Eliminate excessive or duplicate purchases; reduced budget by 14% within one year of taking over purchasing responsibility.
- Seek out new hardware and software to streamline office operations; created a computer network for all administrative support groups and set standard operating procedures to deliver work within aggressive time deadlines.

EXPERIENCE	**TACOMA DESIGN GROUP**, Tacoma, WA *Operations Manager*	1988 - Present
	PAUL K. JONES AGENCY, Bremerton, WA *Administration Officer*	1982 - 1987
	AGFAM MANAGEMENT, Seattle, WA *Manager*	1979 - 1981

EDUCATION	**GRIFFIN COLLEGE**, Seattle, WA Bachelor of Science in Operations Management, May 1979
	PEOPLE IN TRAINING, Yakima, WA Seminars in Public Speaking and Training & Development

REFERENCES	Available upon request.

MARY THOMPSON
4814 Del Ray Avenue
Bethesda, MD 20014
(301) 654 - 1226

EDUCATION

GEORGETOWN UNIVERSITY, Graduate School of Arts & Sciences,
Master of Arts in International Relations, expected May 1994

GEORGETOWN UNIVERSITY
Bachelor of Arts in Economics, May 1989

**TOPICAL
COURSEWORK**

- International Economics
- International Organizations in the Political Arena
- Politics of Global Business
- Asian Law
- Hong Kong in Transition
- U.S./Japan — Politics and Trade

**PROFESSIONAL
EXPERIENCE**

HOWARD UNIVERSITY   **1991 - Present**

Admissions Coordinator
- Organize and implement scheduling process to efficiently process
  financial aid packages.
- Oversee student records and validate applications, with goal of delivering
  materials and funds on a timely basis.
- Prepare personnel and procedural reports for the University Provost's Office.
- Supervise the activities of work study students and intern from other schools.
- Monitor data entry activities performed by 5 clerical staff.
- Manage the automation process and conversion to a new Graduate Aid database.

GEORGETOWN UNIVERSITY   **1989 - 1991**

Admissions Coordinator
- Answered student, alumni, and faculty inquiries regarding various types of
  financial and other resources.
- Met weekly with the Program Director to report on project completion and
  submit updated status reports.

LANGUAGES   Fluent in Korean and Japanese; Proficient in French.

**COMPUTER
SKILLS**
- Use of IBM PCs and Macintosh computers.
- Microsoft Word 5.1
- WordPerfect 5.0
- Aldus Pagemaker
- Aldus Persuasion
- Lotus 1-2-3
- Microsoft Excel
- Harvard Graphics

REFERENCES   Available upon request.

Profession: Admissions Coordinator   Typeface: Helvetica

RICHARD CADARETTE
1620 E. Cliff Road
Burnsville, MN 55337

OBJECTIVE   To utilize over 10 years of proven accomplishments in advertising and public relations to exceed corporate revenue goals.

EXPERIENCE

3/90 - 2/93   **IDS BANK AND TRUST**, Minneapolis, MN
Director - Media Group

- Oversee accounts with budgets up to $3 million, with direct responsibility for 3 managers and 17 support staff.
- Hold weekly staff meetings to coordinate production status, creative materials, and budget requirements.
- Implement media plans for television, radio, and print mediums.
- Meet with clients to propose new marketing strategies and increase advertising budgets; grew existing client revenues by 18% in fiscal 1992.
- Sign-off on all media projects, reporting weekly to corporate senior managers.
- Travel throughout the United States and Europe to meet with clients, attend trade shows, launch new products, and prospect for new accounts.

8/86 - 2/90   **FLANAGAN MEDIA GROUP**, St. Paul, MN
Account Manager

- Handled four of the top five corporate accounts, which contributed over 40% to gross revenues.
- Developed specialized contracts with talent agencies and consultants to maximize efficiencies; reduced monthly expenditures by 7%.
- Represented clients during media negotiations, photoshoots, and recording sessions.
- Participated in the preparation of new business brochures and direct response package sent to Fortune 1000 companies.

7/83 - 5/86   **TXT ENTERPRISES**, Deluth, MN
Assistant Account Coordinator

- Reported to Account Manager representing retail and food service accounts, with responsibility for public relations efforts.
- Developed press releases, contacted media representatives, and distributed materials through all corporate affiliates and to media sources.
- Maintained Microsoft Excel spreadsheets reflecting budgets and current expenditures on over 50 accounts.

EDUCATION   **BOSTON UNIVERSITY**, Boston, MA
Bachelor of Arts in Communications, May 1983
Relevant Coursework: Advertising & Promotions, 20th Century Advertising, Media and Politics, Developing Brand Consciousness, and Direct Response.

COMPUTER SKILLS   Macintosh hardware; various word processing, spreadsheet, and management applications.

INTERESTS   Avid golfer — Regional Tournament Champion, 1989 & 1991.

REFERENCES   Furnished upon request.

Typeface: Times

Profession: Advertising

GARY SACK

12 Deever Street
Flintville, TN 37335
(615) 937 - 0904

**work
history**

POWERS MEDIA GROUP, Chattanooga, TN
1988 - Present

Account Executive
- Implement public relations and marketing campaigns for consumer, financial services, telecommunications, and computer accounts.
- Promote media relations through press materials and newsletters.
- Set up, manage, and coordinate special events.
- Arrange radio and television promotions.
- Initiate direct mail efforts; buy lists, arrange printing of materials, and test lists and weigh results against goal plans.

SOUTHERN MEDIA COLLABORATIVE, Memphis, TN
1985 - 1987

Account Executive
- Conducted seasonal publicity efforts for Maine wreaths; realized 65% increase in sales first year on account and 50% increase second year.
- Developed a special design competition for packaging the "Maine Bear" collection initiated in 1984; grew sales from $120,000 in annual sales to over $2 million within 14 months.
- Assigned to 3 writers with responsibility for national media tours and arranging live, on site, and remote interviews to publicize works.

RAMADA HOTEL DUNWOODY, Atlanta, GA
1982 - 1983

Account Executive
- Worked with division executive to launch aggressive marketing campaign; surpassed goals with hugely successful "It's Only in Atlanta" campaign.
- Increased roomnights and convention business by over 55%.
- Streamlined agency relationships with fee structures based on quantifiable results of campaigns, i.e. revenues, outside media coverage, etc..

**other
experience**

1984
Spent 13 months with spouse in Paris, France through her completion of corporate assignment. Traveled extensively throughout Europe, with particular focus on visiting museums and galleries. Attended over 50 museum exhibitions and 200 gallery shows.

languages

Fluent in French; general understanding of Italian, Spanish, and German.

education

SPELMAN COLLEGE, Atlanta, GA
1982

Bachelor of Arts in Mass Communications
Honors: Dean's List, five semesters

**study
abroad**

UNITED OVERSEAS BANK, Geneva, Switzerland
1980

Intensive program in Public Relations in Banking

activities

Horseback riding, squash, tennis, golf, swimming, and aviation.

Profession: Advertising Executive   Typeface: Helvetica

JAKE SMITH
2498 Emogene Street
Mobile, AL 36606
(205) 476 - 8189

OBJECTIVE   A management position where solid academic and professional experience in architecture will be fully utilized.

EDUCATION   **DECATUR COLLEGE**, Decatur, AL
Bachelor of Architecture, 1988

Relevant Coursework:
- Urban Planning and Design Methods
- Fundamentals of Building Construction
- Environmental Laws and the Architect
- Woodworking Methods of the 18th Century Craftsman
- Drafting I & II
- Model Construction

Study Abroad Program:

Helmit Guhrer
- A three month program as design assistant to architect based in Berlin, Germany. Participated in model construction, site visits, and meetings with corporate and individual clients.

EXPERIENCE   **FEDERAL DESIGNS**, Portland, ME
January 1990 - January 1993
- Work with local agencies and preservation groups to rehabilitate and develop 18th and 19th century structures.
- Manage the approval process, including site proposals, permit requests, zoning requirements, presentations before town boards and area historical societies, and others.
- Maintain historical standards while addressing modern family needs; developed unique building "attachments" to service kitchen and bath requirements without affecting original structure.

SMITH, ARCHITECT, Kittery, ME
1989
- Coordinated contract work on a major 18th century structure in Stratham, New Hampshire.
- Hired crew and supervised total rehabilitation of an important, 14-room farmhouse and 3 outbuildings.
- Rebuilt fireplaces, painted, wallpapered, replaced 2 floors, removed and replaced damaged clapboards, and installed extensive security system throughout buildings and grounds.
- Designed 2,200 sq. ft. art studio for largest barn on property; built separate, attached solar-powered greenhouse.

INTERESTS   Buying and restoring early 18th century structures.

REFERENCES   Portfolio and professional references available upon request.

Profession: Architect   Typeface: New Century Schoolbook

CELIA BUTTONWOOD
36 Green Street
Newbury, MA 01951
(508) 462 - 0837

OBJECTIVE

To gain practical experience in an art related field while completing a Bachelor of Arts degree in Studio Art.

EDUCATION

MASSACHUSETTS COLLEGE OF ART, Boston, MA
Bachelor of Arts; expected graduation in May, 1994
Major: Studio Art
Minor: Computer Design

Study Plans:
• Study Abroad Program scheduled for Fall 1993 semester in Florence, Italy.

RELATED EXPERIENCE

ROXBURY ELEMENTARY SCHOOL, Boston, MA
Internship, Spring 1993
• Taught children's art classes.

MASSACHUSETTS COLLEGE OF ART, Boston, MA
Teacher's Assistant, Fall 1992
• Participated in art related instruction in a first grade classroom.

CAMP PENTLETON, Amherst, NH
Art Counselor, Summer 1991
• Developed a program to teach children at day camp how to use art materials, paint on various surfaces, and design their own t-shirts.

KARAKOW GALLERY, Boston, MA
Gallery Assistant, Spring 1991
• Helped gallery director prepare for a major show of works by the preeminent artist Donald Judd.

HONORS

• Drawing selected for college's permanent collection.
• Dean's List, all semesters
• Won award for poster designed to serve as billboard for a progressive theater in Boston.

LANGUAGES

Semi-fluent in French; learning German and Italian.

PORTFOLIO

Available upon request.

Profession: Art Student   Typeface: Adobe Garamond

SARAH BELTMANSON

Studio: 1018 Madison Avenue, #5B • New York, NY 10028 • (212) 879 - 5167
Home: 47 Old Stone Hill Road • Pound Ridge, NY 10576 • (914) 764 - 2328

EDUCATION:

1988	SCHOOL OF THE MUSEUM OF FINE ARTS, BOSTON B.F.A.
1985	RHODE ISLAND SCHOOL OF DESIGN A.A. in Fine Arts

GROUP EXHIBITIONS:

1991 - 1993	*Montgomery Art Gallery*
1992	*Segal/Benson* — "Figures"
1991	*Aldorf Gallery* — "Stevens Competition"
1991	*Pound Ridge Arts Center* — "Selections from Area Masters"
1989	*Hirschl & Grossman* — "Paintings and Drawings; Selected Works"
1989	*Rhode Island School of Design* — "Museum School Annual Winter Competition"
1988	*Soho/Soho* — "New York Invitational: Contemporary Masters"
1987	*Lexington Spiritualist Center* — "Religion in the 80s: Does it Exist in Painting?"
1987	*Rhode Island School of Design* — "Women, Men, and Art: A Comparative Show"
1985	*Providence Women's Complex* — "Do They Belong? Women and Art Today"

AWARDS:

1992	Wrightsman Travelling Fellowship
1989	1st Place in Painting; Museum School Annual Winter Competition
1985	Women's League Civic Honor for Art Excellence

EMPLOYMENT:

1988 - Present	ARTS STUDENT'S LEAGUE Teaching Assistant
1985 - 1987	PROVIDENCE COOPERATIVE ART GALLERY Independent Art Teacher

PORTFOLIO:

Slides, reviews, and artworks available upon request.

Profession: Artist   Typeface: Caslon 3 Roman

JOSEPH STAV
286 Bellevue Avenue
Newport, RI 02840
(401) 849 - 5538

**SUMMARY
OF SKILLS**

- ❑ Successful professional experience in a banking environment, with knowledge of Customer Service and Retail Banking.
- ❑ Proven ability to interact with clients and handle full service responsibilities.
- ❑ Effective skills in working with management and fellow team members.

**BANKING
EXPERIENCE**

NEWPORT INSTITUTION FOR SAVINGS, Newport, RI
Teller
5/92 - Present

- Processed various types of client transactions, including deposits, check cashing, deposits and withdrawals for savings accounts, mortgage and loan payments, and foreign currency exchanges.
- Performed duties as Head Teller for two months while the Head Teller was on maternity leave.
- Handled customer service and telemarketing duties to cross sell product lines.
- Balanced ATM transactions on a nightly basis.

FLEET BANK, Providence, RI
Teller
6/90 - 4/92

- Process many kinds of customer transactions, such as the sale of travellers cheques, cashiers checks, certified checks, money orders, deposits and withdrawals, and loan payments.
- Received promotion within four months of employment.
- Held a $7,000 signing authority.
- Worked with clients to solve any account discrepancies and resolve problems in the most effective manner for the customer.

LECHMERE, Cambridge, MA
Customer Service
2/88 - 4/90

- Handled all types of credit card, check, and cash transactions.
- Received spot bonus for excellent performance.
- Processed returned merchandise and verified packaging and contents of boxes to credit appropriate refunds.
- Returned merchandise to locations throughout the store.

COMPUTERS   Data entry systems used in retail establishments.

EDUCATION   **PROVIDENCE HIGH SCHOOL, Providence, RI**
Graduate, College Preparatory Program, 1987

REFERENCES   Available upon request.

Profession: Bank Teller   Typeface: Helvetica

ARISTIDE BRUANT
183 Marlborough Street, #3
Boston, MA 02116
(617) 262 - 4300

PROFESSIONAL OBJECTIVE

To contribute over 10 years of proven banking experience specializing in large institutional account management, systems training, and quality assurance.

PROFESSIONAL HISTORY

BANK OF BOSTON, Boston, MA   1982 - PRESENT
Project Analyst — Systems Project Team   *1991 - Present*

- Converting over 100 processes maintained on subsystems, PCs, manual forms, and by service bureaus to a new trust accounting system.
- Troubleshoot all issues for Institutional Trust/Custody, Pension/Employee Benefits, Safekeeping, and Corporate Trust accounts.
- Coordinate in-depth training classes for 80+ trust officers and other personnel located in 4 states.
- Write and monitor 25 scripts for staff in corporate headquarters as well as affiliate banks. Test user knowledge of new system from both trust administration and operations perspectives.

Account Officer   *1987 - 1991*

- Managed 120+ accounts valued at $2.8 billion, including banks, schools, and foundations, realizing over $500,000 in annual fees. Supported 3 junior officers with over 330 accounts with total value at $3.5+ billion.
- Resolved all client concerns related to affiliate areas, including DTC, Corporate Reorganization, Income Collection, Cash Tellers, Vault Operations, and Mutual Funds/Global Custody.
- Headed, concurrent with account responsibilities, in-house data integrity project. Designed, with 2 programmers, all system reports needed to certify accuracy of data pertaining to name and address files, tax, and other required system fields. Delivered weekly certification reports to 2 senior managers.
- Resolved administration issues for conversion to proposed new system of record for departmental assets ($18+ billion).

Institutional Account Administrator   *1982 - 1987*

- Managed over 40 accounts with $1.3 billion in total value, including correspondent banks, universities, state agencies, and non-profits, realizing over $230,000 in annual fees.
- Initiated research project to uncover lost fees for previous three year period. Recovered $90,000 (out of $105,000) in fees and received Professional Recognition Award for superior performance.
- Oversaw supervisor and 5 support staff for option processing and operations support to other officers.

INTERNAL REVENUE SERVICE, Andover, MA   1980 - 1981
Tax Examiner

- Initiated operational procedures to determine tax underreporting. Submitted claims to taxpayers to collect overdue tax obligations and assessed appropriate penalties.

COMPUTER SKILLS

In-depth knowledge of Microsoft Excel, Lotus 1-2-3, Microsoft Word, WordPerfect, Norton Utilities, PageMaker, Quark Express. General knowledge of approximately 15 other software applications.

EDUCATION

BOSTON UNIVERSITY, Boston, MA
Bachelor of Arts in Economics, May 1979
Special Project: 12 credit project for in-depth, 150 page report on alternative investments in fine arts, particularly 19th century American paintings.

JASON WAKEFIELD
508 Lincoln Avenue
Winnetka, IL 60093
(312) 446 - 8038

**CAREER
OBJECTIVE**

To use expertise in carpentry and property maintenance
in a multi-unit setting and manage a prestigious development.

**PROFESSIONAL
EXPERIENCE**

MUNDELEIN COLLEGE, Chicago, IL   **1988 - Present**
Maintenance Supervisor

Supervise all maintenance activities for a large, 100+ unit
complex, with overall responsibility for carpentry, electrical,
and plumbing assignments.

<u>Areas of Expertise:</u>

Carpentry:
- New Dry Wall
- Hanging Cabinets
- Changing Locks
- Flooring
- Installing Tiles
- Repairing Doors

Electrical:
- New Wiring
- Appliance Repair
- Light Fixtures
- New Outlets

Plumbing:
- New Piping
- New Fixture Installation
- Pipe Replacement
- Cleaning Drains

Purchasing:
- Buying Stock
- Filing Expense Reports

COOK COUNTY HOSPITAL, Chicago, IL   **1980 - 1988**
Maintenance Supervisor

Performed all general maintenance assignments including electrical,
plumbing, carpentry, and appliance repair. Oversaw all grounds-
keeping and snow removal jobs.

STRENGTHS
- Very professional, mature, and focused on delivering the
  highest quality service.
- Taking an assignment from inception to completion.
- Providing on-call service to handle any emergencies.
- Experience with a wide variety of tools.
- Always refining abilities and learning new technical skills.

EDUCATION

CHICAGO STATE UNIVERSITY, Chicago, IL   **1979**
Associates Degree in Business Administration,

**TECHNICAL
STUDIES**

Extensive coursework and apprenticeship experience in wiring,
electrical motors, transformers, hydraulic systems, and welding.

HADLEY ZOLPE

600 Canyon Road   Santa Fe, NM 87501

(505) 982 - 8836

EDUCATION

NEW YORK UNIVERSITY, New York, NY
- Bachelors of Science degree in Performing Arts, cum laude, May 1993
  Dance Concentration
- Minor in Photography
- Dean's List

DANCE TRAINING

- Ballet — various techniques
- Modern — Merce Cunningham and Martha Graham techniques
- Jazz — recognized leadership in many forms

ADDITIONAL TRAINING

- Gymnastics
- Aerobics
- Cheerleading
- Marathon Running

CHOREOGRAPHY EXPERIENCE

- Choreographed 3 separate pieces for New York University's
  Dance Ensemble between 1992 and 1993. One piece selected to
  represent New York University at the Eastern Regional Dance
  Competition '93.
- Choreographed performances of the Santa Fe Dance Troupe,
  a marching drill team; won first place in a 1988 competition.
- Active in promoting local groups, with choreography experience
  in hip-hop, dance, and local amateur video productions.

PERFORMANCE EXPERIENCE

- New York University student/faculty performances and concerts.
- Danced in the musical "West Side Story."
- Member of New York University's Dance Company.
- Active touring with high school and college troupes to perform at
  benefits, private events, and inner-city training programs.
- Danced in the Santa Fe Civic Center's opening ceremonies.

JEFFREY MANHEIM
1869 Fairmount Avenue
Dallas, TX 75209
(214) 742 - 3827

PROFESSIONAL **EXPERIENCE**	**FORT WORTH GRANITE & CONSTRUCTION**, Fort Worth/Dallas, TX	**1984 - Present**

Corporate Comptroller

- Manage all accounting for construction firm specializing in Unit Paving, with annual sales of $4 million.
- Handle all accounts payable and receivable for 6 separate checking accounts.
- Work with Internal Revenue Service, accountants, lawyers, and insurance groups on matters ranging from legal claims to workers compensation issues in different states throughout the country.
- Maintain sole signing authority on all accounts, outside of owner, with no set dollar limits.
- Use extensive knowledge of business, in brick, granite, and cobblestone installation for large commercial projects, to deal effectively with project managers and government officials.

Office Manager

- Direct all efforts of one full-time assistant and any temporary staff.
- Issue trial balance and status reports to owner and silent partners on monthly and quarterly basis.
- File all government reports to Federal, state, and local agencies according to varying schedules.
- Meet new and potential clients, promoting company, scheduling meetings, and generating new leads for business.

MANHEIM RECORD SYSTEMS, Dallas, TX   **1983**
Bookkeeper

- Maintained complete control of expenses, payroll, and tax compliance for small businesses and individuals.

MANHEIM IMPORTS, Dallas, TX   **1978 - 1982**
Principal

- Operated business catering to local residents and affluent tourists.
- Ordered weekly inventories across all product lines and maintained bookkeeping records, with sales averaging $300,000 yearly.
- Hired, trained, and supervised all employees working on both a part-time and full-time basis.

EDUCATION   **DALLAS BAPTIST UNIVERSITY**, Dallas, TX
Undergraduate Study Program in Business Administration, 1976 - 1978

H&R BLOCK, Forth Worth, TX
Certification in Tax Preparation, 1982

INTERESTS   Extensive regional and national travel, dancing, and power-walking.

REFERENCES   References and letters of recommendation available upon request.

Profession: Comptroller / Office Manager   Typeface: Palatino

JANE GUNSTON
316 Buncombe Street
Edgefield, SC 29824
(803) 637 - 2993

OBJECTIVE

- To use proven administrative skills and professional accomplishments to further a company's objectives while maximizing efficiencies.

ACCOMPLISHMENTS

- Diversified Planning: As representative to the Community Action Committee, created highly successful programs meeting the needs of multicultural groups with varying agendas.
- Program Development: Award Community Achievement Award for setting up two unique programs in the city which focused on teen involvement and "skills instead of the streets" action plan.
- Fundraising: Initiated program to raise funds for summer employment for inner city youth; gathered religious and community support, wrote press releases and received radio airplay, and developed volunteer committees to process applications for enrollment.
- Education: Recruited experienced software users to volunteer 3 hours per week to train participants on Lotus 1-2-3 and WordPerfect; solicited and received dedicated office space and 11 computer terminals from local business for a work release program.

PROFESSIONAL EXPERIENCE

THE GUNSTON, Edgefield, SC   **1991 - 1993**

Founder/President

Wrote 120 page proposal for inner city support program, detailing needed religious, community, and governmental support. Outlined funding, real estate and equipment, and operating/staff requirements. Realized full acceptance of plan after 3 months of intense negotiations between all involved parties. Received pledges totaling $185,000 from sponsors for summer works program. Trained 350 city youth with special emphasis on computer training and basic office skills.

WOMEN'S CORRECTIONAL CENTER, Woodburn Hills, SC   **1987 - 1990**

Senior Coordinator

Developed long term training program for female prison inmates to develop skills appropriate for the workplace. Funded 2 Macintosh computer terminals and various software programs through corporate sponsorship. Set up works program with corporate sponsor to enable participants to work at entry-level assignments upon release. Placed over 35 participants in a 3 year period. Wrote action plan to incorporate program into other prisons.

FIVE FORKS, Five Forks, SC   **1985 - 1986**

Research Administrator

Managed projects and volunteer staffing needs for ESL research project. Interviewed enrolled students and gathered in-depth findings. Wrote proposal for review by Executive Council. Presented Director with various alternatives for instituting proposals on 3 regional campuses.

EDUCATION

M.Ed.	Administration and Planning Studies, Rock Hill College		1988
B.A.	Political Science, Voorhees College		1984

MARK ENGLISH
33 West Winter Street
Delaware, OH 43015
(614) 369 - 4681

OBJECTIVE

To offer proven restaurant experience to an organization where commitment to quality and satisfying a demanding clientele are paramount concerns.

WORK EXPERIENCE

MAISON JEAN-CHARLES, Delaware, OH
3/92 - Present
Position: *Chef's Assistant*

- Worked through various schedules to handle the dough making and fillings for calzones and other Italian dishes.
- Set up program to monitor portion control and inventory.
- Participated in training classes to learn various garnishing, sautés, and salad presentations.
- Apprenticed in all areas of the kitchen and received honor of becoming primary assistant to well known chef.

THE SHERATON, Boston, MA
1/91 - 1/92
Position: *Sous Chef*

- Concurrent with primary responsibility of sous chef, oversaw 11 other kitchen employees and trained them in kitchen operations.
- Filled out inventory reports and presented daily and weekly lists to general manager for purchasing.

CAPITOL GRILLE, Providence, RI
4/90 - 12/90
Position: *Prep Cook*

- Prepared stocks and salads, set up hot and cold serving stations, and assisted chef as requested.

MILITARY

UNITED STATES ARMY

Honors:
- Good Conduct Medal
- Army Achievement Medal
- Army Accommodation Medal
- Air Assault Badge

EDUCATION

JOHNSON & WALES COLLEGE, Providence, RI
Associate Degree in Culinary Arts, May 1991

REFERENCES

Professional references and numerous letters of recommendation available upon request.

Profession: Cook / Chef's Assitant　　*Typeface: Helvetica*

BRIAN HAMMIL
481 1st Avenue North, #8
Minneapolis, MN 55403
(612) 339 - 4770

EDUCATION **AUGSBURG COLLEGE**, Minneapolis, MN
M.S. in Rehabilitation Counseling, 1989

UNIVERSITY OF MASSACHUSETTS, Boston, MA
B.S. in Human Services, 1987

CERTIFICATES *Chemical Substances: Use and Abuse*
Certified Home Health Assistance
AIDS Awareness & Prevention
First Aid/CPR
Battered Women in an Urban Environment
Minority Services

WORK
EXPERIENCE **UNIVERSITY OF MINNESOTA**   1989 - Present
HOSPITAL AND CLINIC, Minneapolis, MN
Counselor
- Participated in group counseling sessions on topics ranging from teen violence and academic goal setting to AIDS and public health issues.
- Taught health classes, with particular attention to nutrition development.
- Developed adolescents' domestic skills through weekly training, including setting weekly budgets, food shopping, maintaining order and cleanliness in the home, and other skills to affect one's personal environment.

BOSTON CITY HOSPITAL, Boston, MA   1987 - 1989
Counselor
- Handle counseling at a community hospital day care program for at risk adolescent males.
- Provide skills assessment, development and training, and community integration functions.
- Implement programs to achieve and individual's plan goals.

OTHER
EXPERIENCE **OUTWARD BOUND**, Camden, ME   Summer 1986
Volunteer
- Cleared paths for seasonal use by tourists and area residents.

AFFILIATIONS *Member, National Association of Alternative Drug Therapies*
Member, Boy Scouts of America
Member, Minneapolis Choral Group

LANGUAGES Bilingual in Spanish and English.

REFERENCES Professional references available upon request.

CARLA SAMPSON
9282 S.W. Gemini Drive
Beaverton, OR 97005
(503) 641 - 0820

**CAREER
GOAL**

To contribute in a health care or day care environment where proven skills and accomplishments would be fully utilized.

SUMMARY

- 7 years experience working with children between the ages of three and seven.
- Proven strength working with children from various cultural and socioeconomic backgrounds.
- Administrative and computer skills needed to process any government and agency forms.
- Excellent leadership skills, developing programs where parents participate in childhood development.

**DIRECT
EXPERIENCE**

JACK 'N JILL SCHOOL, Portland, OR   **1991 - Present**
Day Care Coordinator
- Maintained overall responsibility for eighteen children ranging in age from three to five years.
- Supervise staff of two and develop day plans for indoor and outdoor activities.
- Set up alliance with Elder Care Living Center; initiated program where elders may participate twice each week in planned activities, including visits to their center.

PORTLAND HOSPITAL, Portland, OR   **1989 - 1990**
Translator — Emergency Ward
- Performed a variety of administrative duties, such as translating documents for parents of patients, completing applications, and acting as interpreter for other staff.
- Explained health care issues and reviewed various care options such as hospitalization and out-patient services.
- Helped administrators set up play room for visiting families and patients.

YOUTH COUNCIL NETWORK, Hillsboro, OR   **1988**
Youth Coordinator
- Developed a program to access area resources for teenagers, with particular emphasis on "Project Adventure," a skills building program which develops athletic skills, team building, and nature conservancy.

**OTHER
EXPERIENCE**

JONES PLACEMENT GROUP, Portland, OR   **1986 - 1987**
Administrative Assistant
- Met with clients and processed applications and information.
- Completed data entry assignment to record over 5,000 names, addresses, and client statistics for a sales force.
- Typed correspondence for 3 managers.

LANGUAGES

Fluency in Spanish

SEMINARS

- Personal Development in a Youth Services Environment
- Effective Day Care Strategies
- Introduction to WordPerfect and Lotus 1-2-3

Profession: Day Care / Youth Services   Typeface: New Century Schoolbook

LILA COGAN
210 Hickory Street
Scranton, PA 18505
(717) 346 - 6536

OBJECTIVE

To utilize over 15 years of proven leadership skills to support an aggressive business owner in developing market share in service or retail businesses.

AREAS OF EXPERTISE

o   Proven experience building long term relationships with clients.
o   Generating new business relationships which achieve revenue growth for the corporation.
o   Spotting new trends and introducing new and streamlined services to the marketplace.
o   Assessing client priorities according to market trends in order to maximize product identity and turnover at retail level.
o   Resolving client concerns and problems with a partnership approach to client needs.

WORK EXPERIENCE

MONROE COURIER, Scranton, PA
General Manager
(1988 - Present)
•   Control all activities of a busy courier service with responsibility for managing personnel, opening new accounts, building client relationships, and growing market share.

COGAN TIES, Pittsburgh, PA
Sales Manager
(1984 - 1988)
•   Developed and grew a prosperous tie cart business and put together a plan to sell as franchise to investors.

WICKED FAST COURIER SERVICE, Boston, MA
District Sales Manager
(1978 - 1983)
•   Succeeded in expanding courier business and opening new markets, with increases over 25% per year over a 5 year period.

JOURNAL GRAPHICS, Hartford, CT
Training Coordinator
(1975 - 1978)
•   Trained new recruits on cold-calling techniques to sell space advertising to area and regional businesses.

VOLUNTEER ACTIVITIES

BETHANY COMMUNITY GROUP, Bethany, PA
Chairperson
(1989 - 1992)
•   Develop programs to beautify area and host special events for families throughout region.

INTERESTS

Hiking, boating, and participation in monthly mock debating events.

Profession: Delivery Manager / Owner   Typeface: Adobe Garamond

GOLDIE HARMON

Local Address:	*Permanent Address:*
10 St. Stephens Way	1840 Fern Palm Drive
Orlando, FL 32816	Edgewater, FL 32141

EDUCATION

UNIVERSITY OF CENTRAL FLORIDA, Orlando, FL
Bachelor of Science degree in Business Administration and Fashion Merchandising
Expected graduation, May 1994

Related Coursework:

- ▲ History of Fashion
- ▲ Display and Design
- ▲ Principles of Line & Color
- ▲ Retail Design
- ▲ Fashion Merchandising
- ▲ European Textiles

INTERNSHIP EXPERIENCE

VANESSA'S, Daytona Beach, FL   Spring 1992
Fashion Assistant
- Helped set up swatch books for designer to use in making client presentations.
- Answered correspondence and wrote to importers and exporters to obtain information regarding range of services offered.
- Scheduled work assignments between designer, manufacturers, and others.
- Learned to use Microsoft Works and access extensive clip art file in order to create reports and presentations.

WORK EXPERIENCE

SOUTHERN REPUBLIC, Miami, FL   Fall 1992 - Present
Sales Associate
- Create store displays and help prepare for fashion shows held in this exclusive retail shop.
- Coordinate outfits and accessories for clients and suggest ways to develop wardrobe.
- Participate in semi-annual inventories and help design special promotions to move certain items.

LAUDERDALE'S, Ft. Lauderdale, FL   Spring 1992 - Fall 1992
Sales Associate
- Set up counter and table displays to generate additional sales of accessories.
- Processed all types of transactions, including cash, check, and credit card orders.

SKILLS
- Extensive experience in creating fashion illustrations.
- Excellent dressmaking abilities; created and sold over 50 dresses while in high school and college.

COMPUTERS   Macintosh, Microsoft Works, and design files maintained on system.

REFERENCES   Portfolio with slides, dress designs, and finished samples available upon request.

Profession: Designer's Assistant   Typeface: Helvetica

JOHN WYATT
265 North Street
Bennington, VT 05201
(802) 442 - 3373

OBJECTIVE Utilizing strong academic experience to contribute to a position as an apprentice in an firm specializing in architectural design.

EDUCATION **UNIVERSITY OF CHICAGO, Chicago, IL**
Bachelor of Architecture, May 1990
Relevant Coursework: Concrete and Steel Construction; Estimation for Government Buildings, Drafting, C.A.D., Planning for the Urban Environment, and Contemporary Design.

DePAUL UNIVERSITY, Chicago, IL
Intensive 6-month program studying the designs and practices of Frank Lloyd Wright.

SCHOOL OF THE MUSEUM OF FINE ARTS, Boston, MA
Undergraduate studies in Graphic Design and Computer Imaging

INTERNSHIP **German S.A.S. Enterprises, Inc.**
Work Assistant

- Aided in the residential design division for this international architecture firm.
- Assigned to 3 designers and performed various tasks as assigned.
- Worked full-time schedule both in department and on-site with designers.

EXPERIENCE **AMERICAN DESIGNS, INC., Portland, ME**   1991 - 1992
Designer

- Designed for the renovated interior and exterior of a 16-room Victorian mansion.
- Applied for and received all necessary building permits.
- Presented specifications at community hearing to remove community restrictions established for district; received all concessions.
- Helped hire woodworking and paint crews for 3-month project.
- Oversaw interior and exterior construction and finishing for 2 crews totaling 7 workers.
- Coordinated open house for civic leaders and area businesses.
- Received full-page write-up in regional paper and subsequent offer to write quarterly column on design and repair issues.

NORTHEAST JOURNAL, Augusta, ME   1989 - 1991
Columnist

- Wrote 4 stories on the design and repair problems facing owners of early American homes. Articles included:
  - "The Keeping Room: What to Keep in it Now?"
  - "How to Choose the 4 Different Paints for Your Victorian Mansion"
  - "Modern Conveniences: Designs for the Early American Home"
  - "Carpet versus Wood Flooring: My Opinion"

SYSTEM SKILLS C.A.D. (3 years); Adobe Photoshop (2 years); Microsoft Word (1 year); One year of extensive use of Macintosh hardware, black & white and color printers, scanners (hand held and flatbed), and CD-ROM (with emphasis on design).

LANGUAGES Proficiency in French.

INTERESTS Frank Lloyd Wright; Member of Augusta Planning Commission; Drawing; Baseball

REFERENCES Portfolio (slides or photoprints) and letters of recommendation available upon request.

Typeface: Helvetica

Profession: Designer / Architect

MARY STOCKWELL
16 East 57th Street
New York, NY 10022
(212) 753 - 1872

PROFESSIONAL OBJECTIVE

To utilize proven academic and professional experience to contribute to the personnel division of a progressive company.

SUMMARY OF QUALIFICATIONS

✓ High level executive with a successful track record in creating and implementing personnel programs while cutting corporate expenses.
✓ Over 4 years experience as a personnel manager, with proven expertise in resolving employee issues and maximizing efficiencies for company.
✓ Strong problem solving abilities, with excellent communication and interpersonal skills needed to cultivate and maintain effective employee relations.
✓ Use of fluency in three languages to participate in training programs developed to address multicultural and socioeconomic concerns.

PROFESSIONAL EXPERIENCE

CHEMICAL BANK, New York, NY   1986 - Present
Division Executive
• Led overhaul process of personnel division, managing the updating of job descriptions, evaluations process, and personnel files for over 4,000 employees.
• Conducted resource interviews with over 60 division managers to develop in-house training programs focusing on office automation.
• Set policies and procedures for employee relations and labor review.
• Presented paper entitled "Organizational and Psychological Phenomena Relevant to Organizations" to senior management. Paper outlined courses of action to build skill sets which enable organizations to succeed against national and international competition.

R.H. MACY, New York, NY   1980 - 1986
Division Manager
• Participated in executive training, performance evaluation, and follow-up meetings.
• Completed data charts to determine salary ranges for department with 1,200 employees.
• Worked with senior project team to develop a job resource analysis program encompassing skills review, interviewing, and relocation of displaced workers.

EDUCATION

SIMMONS COLLEGE, Boston, MA
Bachelor of Science in Psychology, cum laude, 1978
Minor: Business Administration
Dean's List

L'UNIVERSITA DEGLI STUDI DI SIENA, Siena, Italy
Study Abroad Program, 1977
Emphasis: Intensive Italian language instruction.

LANGUAGES

Fluent in Italian, Spanish, and English; proficiency in French and German.

PERSONAL DATA

✓ Single
✓ Willing to relocate, both nationally and internationally
✓ Abstract painter, participating in solo and group exhibitions in New York, Chicago, Bonn, and Geneva.
✓ Gourmet cook, with three month apprenticeship with Michel Bras in Laguiole, France, France Premier Chef of the Year.
✓ Extensive travel experience throughout Europe and the United States; eight month safari and travel through various African countries.

REFERENCES

Professional, academic, and gallery references available upon request.

Profession: Division Executive   Typeface: Bookman

SARAH WRIGHTSMAN
602 Brighton Drive
Bloomingdale, IL 60108
(708) 351 - 2269

**TEACHING
EXPERIENCE**
    ARLINGTON HEIGHTS HIGH SCHOOL, Arlington Heights, IL   Fall 1992
Administrative Assistant
- Assisted in the preparation of an annual report and brochures highlighting special school programs developed to address multicultural environment.

    NORTH PARK ELEMENTARY SCHOOL, Chicago, IL   Spring 1992
Student Teacher
- Provided assistance to English teacher for inner-city students, ages six through nine years. Taught as a substitute teacher in teacher's absence. Helped to implement an "Adopt a Book" program with emphasis on picking classic works from many cultures.

    JOSEPH WOODS DAY SCHOOL, Chicago, IL   Winter 1991/1992
Student Teacher
- Supervised over 30 children in an art class. Participated in instructing children in painting, drawing, ceramics, and clay sculpture.

    SAUNDERS LANGUAGE INSTITUTE, Chicago, IL   Fall 1991
Receptionist
- Performed data entry assignments, organized office, and answered telephones for this private language instruction school. Assisted in various special projects.

    CAMP AVATAR, Ellis Grove, IL   Summer 1990
Camp Counselor
- Supervised arts and crafts activities, swimming events, and other sports activities for the kindergarten cabin.
- Organized night trips and hiking events for up to 25 children.

**OTHER
EXPERIENCE**
    LERNERS, Chicago, IL   Fall 1990 - Winter 1992
Sales Associate   (Part-Time)
- Worked in Bed Linens with responsibility for setting up special displays and designing space to hold maximum amount of goods while allowing for ease of shopping.
- Helped shoppers with selecting bed linens and suggesting other accessories for purchase.

SKILLS
    Art — Extensive coursework in all media, with special emphasis on ceramics and painting.

    Computers — Solid knowledge of many graphic software applications, including Quark Express, Adobe Illustrator, Adobe Photoshop, as well as hardware to support production (scanners, etc.).

EDUCATION
    COLUMBIA COLLEGE, Chicago, IL
Bachelor of Science in Elementary Education, May 1993

CERTIFICATION
    Illinois Certification (1 - 6)
American Red Cross Standard First Aid and CPR

REFERENCES
    Furnished upon request.

NANCY MAINE

8000 Leesburg Pike, #11
Falls Church, VA 22043
(703) 356 - 0835

PROFESSIONAL OBJECTIVE	To build upon a proven track record of corporate event planning and sales to meet the aggressive goals of a demanding company.

EXPERIENCE

HYATT REGENCY WASHINGTON, Washington, DC   **10/88 - Present**
Sales Executive — Corporate Events

- Achieved prospecting goals of 35 contacts per week, resulting in personal visits to over 15 potential corporate accounts and signing 50% to business function contracts.
- Exceeded revenue quotas by 120%, maintaining top position in office out of 7 other sales executives.
- Recognized as Top Sales Performer all four years with company, outperforming other staff by at least 35%.
- Developed relationships with government, non-profit, and community groups to create and coordinate highly profitable functions for small groups.
- Set up highly specialized medical conferences to attract international attention and participation.

THE JEFFERSON HOTEL, Washington, DC   **4/85 - 9/88**
Function Coordinator

- Developed and implemented comprehensive function packages catering to individual and corporate foreign travelers.
- Wrote procedures manual to outline responsibility of staff in running all facets of event, such as media releases, sponsored area events, activity plans, and menus targeted to particular markets.
- Participated in marketing campaign designed to grow segment of business by 75%; realized a 200% increase in business within 15 months.

THE HAY-ADAMS HOTEL, Washington, DC   **1/82 - 4/85**
Assistant Manager
- Transferred to new region to participate in training program focusing on functions and events development.
- Assisted division managers in setting expansion strategies to gain market share; increased roomnights by 28% within eight months.

BOSTON PARK PLAZA HOTEL & TOWERS, Boston, MA   **9/80 - 11/81**
Assistant Manager
- Participated in extensive training program with rotations through all the divisions of the hotel.

INTERNSHIPS

LE MERIDIEN, Boston, MA   **Summer 1978**
Intern

EDUCATION

BOSTON UNIVERSITY, Boston, MA
Bachelor of Arts in Business Administration, cum laude, May 1979

COMPUTERS SKILLS

Macintosh (4 years); Microsoft Word (4 years), Quark Express (2 years).

INTERESTS

Extensive worldwide travel, skiing, and art exhibitions.

REFERENCES

Available upon request.

MARY ZOETROPE
712 E. Main Street
Lexington, KY 40508
(606) 231 - 6592

CAREER OBJECTIVE

Seeking a position in a progressive company where proven skills
will be fully utilized and developed.

EDUCATION

MERCHANTS COLLEGE, Portland, ME   **May 1991**
Associate Degree in Merchandising
Minor: Textile Manufacturing

Related Coursework:
★   Merchandising/Buying
★   Textiles of India
★   Line and Design
★   Space Advertising in Alternative Media
★   Fashion Retailing
★   Window Displays
★   Corporate Promotions — Seasons and Strategies
★   Manufacturing and Importation of Goods

WORK EXPERIENCE

TEXTILE MILL OF NEW HAMPSHIRE, Conway, NH   **1992 - Present**
Staff Assistant

•   Act as primary support person to senior textile designer,
    contacting companies, setting up appointments for reviewing
    textiles, and arranging meetings with overseas contacts.
•   Track various contracts on Macintosh computer using
    Microsoft Excel. Input all figures for all contracts and submit
    bi-weekly reports for management review.
•   Operate multi-party telephones, file reports, photocopy
    bids and contracts, and perform other office assignments
    as required.

HOWARD FINNEY, INC., Portland, ME   **1991**
Secretary

•   Handled all office support functions for 6-person office,
    including photocopying, answering telephones, faxing
    documents, and various word processing assignments.

SYSTEM SKILLS

IBM: WordPerfect 5.1
Macintosh: Microsoft Excel

REFERENCES

Available upon request.

LAUREN ACKERMANN
501 Cliff Street, #6
Santa Cruz, CA 95060
(408) 427 - 8925

OVERVIEW
- Proven ability to achieve academic goals while gaining valuable sales experience in fashion through both internship and work experience.
- Working with managers to learn how to set up schedules and appointments with buyers, clients, and representatives from corporate accounts.
- Successful team player, organizing displays and marketing programs and setting group goals to achieve revenue projections.

EDUCATION

LOS ANGELES TECHNICAL INSTITUTE, Los Angeles, CA
Associates Degree in Applied Science, May 1991
Major in Fashion Merchandising

Relevant Coursework:

- Fashion Merchandising
- Fashion Show Productions
- Computer Systems - An Overview
- Using a Database in Merchandising
- Display & Design
- Business Administration
- Operations Management
- Retail Operations

Activities:

- Student Services Representative — Responded to student inquiries, helped with the orientation process, and prepared and processed candidates for graduation.

SANTA CRUZ COMMUNITY COLLEGE, Santa Cruz, CA
Adult Continuing Education Program, Summers 1987 - 1991
- Fashion Sales (3 credits)
- Setting up a Business (1 credit)
- Market Cycles in Fashion Merchandising (3 credits)

EXPERIENCE

SCOTTS VALLEY FASHIONS, Scotts Valley, CA
Sales Associate, Summer 1991
- Handled the merchandising of stock, assisted customers in item selection, coordinated seasonal displays, and set up special point of purchase displays.

GLENDALE LEGAL SERVICES, INC., Glendale, CA
Secretary, 1990 - 1991 (Part-Time)
- Answered telephones, filed and updated documents, and performed billing processes according to regulatory procedures.

ACTIVITIES
Girl Scout Leader — California Council Member
Board Member — Santa Cruz Civic Group
Volunteer — Santa Cruz Community Group

REFERENCES
Available upon request.

Profession: Fashion / Retail Sales   Typeface: Helvetica

S T E L L A   R O P E S
119 East Charlotte Street
Millersville, PA 17551
(717) 872 - 3692

SUMMARY OF STRENGTHS	o Over 9 years of professional experience as a flight attendant with American Airlines. o Excellent interpersonal and communications skills, with particular strength in public speaking and group presentations. o Strong writing abilities, with experience putting together training programs and media kits to represent airline. o Proven abilities in training and supervision, promoting personal growth and development. o Fluency in four languages.

WORK HISTORY

AMERICAN AIRLINES, Philadelphia, PA   **1983 - Present**
Flight Attendant

- Organize the inflight services for passengers on both national and international flights.
- Complete safety and complaint reports for management review.
- Develop training programs to develop the skills of new flight attendants.
- Contact guest speakers and arrange for special seminars focusing on strengthening interpersonal skills and handling crisis situations.
- Demonstrate passenger safety procedures.

LAGERFELD & AQUILON, Philadelphia, PA   **1981 - 1983**
Account Executive

- Consistently achieved top-biller status with emphasis on new business.
- Assisted in hiring and training new account executives.
- Created promotional campaigns for both retail and agency accounts.

FORD LAFAVORE, INC., Philadelphia, PA   **Fall 1980**
Office Coordinator

- Supported general manager and seven salespeople in all phases of office administration.
- Supervised 3 clerical staff.

EDUCATION

XAVIER UNIVERSITY, Cincinnati, OH
Bachelor of Science, 1980
Concentration: Public Relations

Activities:
- Participated in the University's Student Legal Advisor Program. Advised students charged with misconduct as to their rights within the University hearing process. Ensured proper hearing for the charged student.

LANGUAGES   Fluent in French, Spanish, Japanese, and English.

AFFILIATIONS
o American Airlines Training Committee
o American Airlines "Train the Trainer" Program
o Member & Volunteer, Philadelphia Museum of Art
o Member & Volunteer, American Red Cross

REFERENCES   Available upon request.

Profession: Flight Attendant   Typeface: Palatino

ANNA PRATT
140 Dahlonega Street, No. 17
Cumming, Georgia 30130

(404) 889 - 1643

11/91 - Present

APPLE CORE, INC., Atlanta, GA

Stationery & Packaging
Design Manager

> Product Development

> Design/Comps/Prototypes/Mechanicals/Production

> Promotional Materials

Exhibitions
Art Coordinator

> Exhibit Design

> Brochure Development

> Media Releases

> Photography

10/86 - 10/91

FISHER MEDIA GROUP, Marietta, GA

Food Products
Designer

> Label Design & Production

> Product Illustrations

> Copywriting

THE MUSEUM SCHOOL
The Museum of Fine Arts, Boston
BFA, Graphic Design
1985

Profession: Graphic Designer   Typeface: Adobe Garamond

ANITA SANTANIELLO
5000 Pearl East Circle
Boulder, CO 80301
(303) 786 - 1158

GOAL   To utilize proven skills and experience in hair salons to contribute
to the long term growth of a progressive salon.

**WORK
HISTORY**   **VEX SALONS**, Longmont, CO   **6/91 - Present**
Manager

- Staff the salon and supervise performance of 8 employees.
- Handle inventory control and order stock on a weekly basis.
- Reconcile daily receipts and make night deposits.
- Work with owner to develop marketing campaigns.
- Train new employees.
- Contact experts to conduct seminars in various aspects of hair care.

THE ULTIMATE ADVANTAGE, Greeley, CO   **5/90 - 5/91**
Manager
- Ran all operations for a busy salon with 9 employees and 3 consultants.
- Reported to absentee owners on a weekly basis all aspects of receipts
  and expenses.
- Used Macintosh computer and Microsoft Excel to generate detailed
  cost accountings on a bi-weekly basis.
- Set up tracking lists used to contact clients, build additional sales,
  and send out regular press releases.

PICK 'N PAY, Avondale, CO   **3/87 - 2/90**
Assistant Manager
- Received and verified all inventory for convenience store/service station.
- Supervised shifts and scheduled employees.
- Participated in company training programs to build skills.
- Received 5 recognition awards for superior performance.

EDUCATION   **AVONDALE HIGH SCHOOL**, Avondale, CO   **1987**
Graduate, College Preparatory Program

COLORADO SPRINGS BEAUTY GROUP, Colorado Springs, CO   **1989**
Salon Management Certificate

DALE CARNEGIE SEMINAR, Aurora, CO   **1991**
Certificate

COMPUTERS   General knowledge of Macintosh computers as well as word processing and
spreadsheet applications.

OTHER DATA   Dual citizenship in the United States and Italy.

REFERENCES   Furnished upon request.

EMILY STANHOPE
7794 E. Osie Street, #5
Wichita, KS 67207
(316) 685 - 4481

HIGHLIGHTED STRENGTHS

- Excellent organizational and interpersonal skills.
- Proven abilities dealing with clients in a service setting.
- Detail oriented professional successful at seeing projects through to completion.
- Multilingual, with strong intercultural communications experience.

PROFESSIONAL EXPERIENCE

WICHITA HOTEL, Wichita, KS   6/89 - Present
Office Manager (11/89 - Present)

- Supervise the housekeeping and maintenance staff, with responsibility for determining daily assignments, preparing reports for management, and reviewing status of all work.
- Work directly with clients and travel agents to book reservations and sell tour company packages.
- Handle the checking in and checking out process, verifying reservations using computer system.
- Settle daily account balances and file weekly reports to corporate management.
- Resolve client discrepancies and negotiate discounts as appropriate.

Front Desk Manager (6/89 - 10/89)

- Assigned to front desk to train new manager on generating computer reports, running credit checks, and maintaining room inventory.
- Participated in review program affecting concierge desk, information center, and reservation department.

TOPEKA CONVENTION COMPLEX, Topeka, KS   1/88 - 5/89
Planning Assistant

- Assisted manager in the planning and coordination of recreational and educational events for community service group.
- Prepared flyers and special event brochures sent to area newspapers, agencies, and television stations.
- Organized storage areas for donations and equipment needed to refurbish area parks and public access areas.
- Maintained records for expenditures; delivered spreadsheet report to accountant on a monthly basis.

COMPUTERS   IBM PCs; Windows, Lotus 1-2-3, WordPerfect 5.1.

EDUCATION   **UNIVERSITY OF KANSAS**, Kansas City, KS   1986 - 1987
Undergraduate studies in Business

LANGUAGES   Fluent in Spanish and French; reading ability in German and Italian.

PERSONAL DATA

- Willing to relocate, both nationally and internationally.
- Extensive worldwide travel; educated (2 years) in Spain, with frequent

Profession: Hotel Administration   *Typeface: Adobe Garamond*

HOWARD BEND
46921 Bayside Parkway, Loft #3
Fremont, CA 94538
(510) 657 - 4409

STRENGTHS

- Proven administrative and operations management expertise in the areas of staff training and building programs which increase profitability.
- Active involvement with both national and international affiliates, developing special promotions such as weekend packages, area event packages, and other programs to increase roomnights.
- Developing training programs for staff to translate client interests into increased sales quotas and higher net profits.
- Implementing streamlined operations which have increased net margins by over 8% within a 10-month time frame.

PROFESSIONAL EXPERIENCE

SAN JOSE HOTELS & CONVENTION CENTER, San Jose, CA   **1986 - Present**
Director of Front Office Operations
- Manage a staff totaling 60, with responsibility for five departments within the Front Office.
- Prepare Rooms Forecast, Expense Reports, Payroll and Expense Reports, and Quality Control Analysis on a monthly basis for senior management.
- Wrote 80-page Standard Operating Procedures manual for all Front Office departments, resulting in streamlined operations and reducing expenses by 12%.
- Implement incentive programs based upon set performance standards; realized a first year payout of $28,000 and overall savings to corporation of $80,000.
- Develop promotions, working with creative department to prepare ad copy, pricing information, layouts, and incentive offers to achieve immediate returns.
- Teach seminars throughout the United States to corporate affiliates, with a primary focus of eliminating redundant service procedures and creating workflows that maximize efficiencies.

HYATT REGENCY, Los Angeles, CA   **1979 - 1986**
Supervisor of Front Office Operations (1984 - 1986)
- Set up individual and corporate programs to increase market share and build stable, repeat client base.
- Grew corporate accounts from 35 to 180 within a year and a half with corresponding increase in revenues of 40%.
- Received Corporate Recognition Award as Outstanding Leader in New Business Development, an honor given to one manager yearly out of 28 hotels.

Manager, Staff Development Program (1979 - 1983)
- Over a two year period, rotated throughout all departments of hotel, with primary responsibility of learning all office functions and assisting department heads with all supervision and management duties.

SHERATON GRANDE, Los Angeles, CA   **1978**
Management Training Program

EDUCATION

CALIFORNIA STATE UNIVERSITY, Long Beach, CA   **1977**
Bachelor of Science in Hospitality Administration

LANGUAGES

Fluent in Spanish; Proficient in Portuguese.

AFFILIATIONS

Hotel Marketing Association

References Available Upon Request

VANESSA T. COLE
14 Ross Hill Road
Lisbon, CT 06351
(203) 376 - 5814

GOAL	Utilizing over fourteen years of proven leadership experience as an Account Executive to contribute to the insurance field.

**WORK
HISTORY**

HARTFORD MUTUAL INSURANCE COMPANY, Hartford, CT
Account Manager (1990 - Present)

- Handle a book of business with premium value over $2.5 million.
- Conduct a wide variety of management functions, producing substantial new production yearly.

AMERI-LIFE COMPANY, New York, NY
Account Executive (1984 - 1989)

- Increased premium volumes from $800,000 to $1.4 million, with overall responsibility for marketing, production, and servicing of a wide range of insurance products.
- Marketed product lines to service the needs of manufacturing companies, financial institutions, retail establishments, and other major firms.

STEPHENS, JOHNSON & FORTUNA, New York, NY
Account Executive (1980 - 1984)

- Managed a staff of six with responsibility for marketing new products and supervising various lines of insurance.
- Supervised underwriting and clerical functions.
- Converted multiple accounts into one primary account; achieved 35% in operational efficiencies.

EDUCATION

BROWN UNIVERSITY, Providence, RI
Master of Arts in Business Administration, 1983

BROWN UNIVERSITY, Providence, RI
Bachelor of Arts in English, 1980

BROWN INSTITUT DE PARIS, Paris, France
Study Abroad Program in France, Fall 1978

**CERTIFICATES
& LICENSES**

- Property and Casualty Underwriter, Connecticut Registration
- Licensed Insurance Broker in Connecticut and Rhode Island
- Property and Casualty Underwriter Instructor, registered in Connecticut
- Connecticut Real Estate License #3824870

REFERENCES   Available upon request.

Profession: Insurance Executive   Typeface: Times

STANLEY MUSKER
2816 Clematis Street
Sarasota, FL 34239
(813) 365 - 1172

**GEOGRAPHICAL
PREFERENCE**   London; Paris; Geneva; Tokyo

EDUCATION   **BOSTON UNIVERSITY**, Boston, MA   **May 1991**
                  Bachelor of Arts in International Relations
                  Regional Track: East Asia
                  Topical Track: International Business & Economics

                  Related Coursework:
                  v   Contemporary East Asian Economics
                  v   Principles of International Marketing
                  v   International Monetary Banking
                  v   International Law in Developing Nations
                  v   Foreign Policies as Affected by the United States
                  v   Culture and Society of East Asia
                  v   Europe in the 90s
                  v   Socialism, Communism, and Free Market Trade

**WORK
EXPERIENCE**   **MARKS WORLDWIDE DISTRIBUTORS**, Sarasota, FL   **3/93 - Present**
                  Account Executive
                  • Open new accounts through telemarketing, mailings, and meeting
                    directly with clients.
                  • Determine currency fluctuations and their effects on bid proposals.
                  • Work with senior staff to buy and sell currencies in local foreign
                    exchange markets.

                  FULLER & THOMPSON, Houston, TX   **9/92 - 2/93**
                  Marketing Assistant
                  • Performed investigations of competition's pricing and promotions
                    strategies; presented findings to senior managers on a weekly basis.
                  • Helped launch new product which gained 35% increase in sales within
                    two months of launch.
                  • Worked with account managers to implement aggressive strategies to
                    gain market share for client's products.

                  CLAIBOURNE PARTNERS, New York, NY   **Winter 1991 - Summer 1992**
                  Assistant Manager
                  • Handled incoming merchandise and created selling floor arrangements.
                  • Prepared weekly schedules and compiled employee payroll data.
                  • Processed daily accounting receipts.
                  • Supervised employees in store manager's absence.

COMPUTERS   Over 3 years proven experience with both Macintosh and IBM computers;
                  excellent abilities with Lotus 1-2-3, Microsoft Office, Pagemaker, and other
                  applications.

LANGUAGES   Fluent in Japanese, Cantonese, French, and Spanish.

INTERESTS   Graphic applications of the Macintosh computer; competitive squash and
                  tennis; world travel.

REFERENCES   Available upon request.

Profession: International Marketing   Typeface: Palatino

MICHAEL DeLUCA
160 Townsend Street, #6
San Francisco, CA 94107
(415) 243 - 6107

EDUCATION

UNIVERSITY OF SAN FRANCISCO, San Francisco, CA
Bachelor of Arts in Spanish, May 1989
Graduated magna cum laude; GPA 3.65/4.00

Relevant Coursework:
- Spanish Grammar
- Survey of Spanish Literature
- Renaissance Spain - An Exploratory
- Picasso and Barcelona
- Modern Spanish Thought
- Post-War Spanish Fiction
- Post-War Political Thought
- Guernica — A Critical Analysis

INSTITUTE OF SPANISH STUDIES, Barcelona, Spain
Study Abroad Program in Spanish Language and Spanish Art, Spring 1988

HONORS

Dean's List, all semesters
National Scholastic Honor Society
Who's Who Among Students in American Universities & Colleges
Student Representative for Development Office

LANGUAGES

Fluent in Spanish, with over nine years of in-depth studies in verbal and written communication in the Spanish language. Extensive knowledge of classic Spanish literature and post-war Spanish political thought.

Solid understanding of German, Italian, and French.

WORK EXPERIENCE

GOLDEN GATE UNIVERSITY, San Francisco, CA   10/92 - Present
Administrator
- Work with community focus groups to define curriculum for new Spanish arts program.
- Meet with student and faculty panels to review subject areas under consideration, texts to be used, and teaching methods under consideration.
- Report findings to language department head and suggest methods for program implementation.

THE COMMUNITY PROJECT, Los Angeles, CA   8/90 - 9/92
ESL Teacher
- Taught English to children and adults enrolled in aggressive six week programs; participants attended 8 total sessions, each with a separate focus.
- Created learning program highlighting Spanish painting, literature, and culture.

DAMIA GALLERIES, San Francisco, CA   6/89 - 7/90
Gallery Assistant
- Helped organize shows for this gallery specializing in the works of Cuban and Mexican artists.
- Worked with owner to put together 2 exhibition catalogs.

AFFILIATIONS

California Cultural Group, Co-Chair

REFERENCES

Transcripts: Career Services, University of San Francisco, San Francisco, CA.
Professional references available upon request.

Profession: Language Instructor   Typeface: Adobe Garamond

DAVID BARRETT
3287 Rosendale Road
Schenectady, NY 12309
(518) 783 - 8155

**MILITARY
EXPERIENCE**

UNITED STATES MARINE CORPS
1988 - 1992

Section Leader/Team Leader
- Conducted a unit specializing in demolitions, infantry and anti-armor tactics.
- Taught weekly classes to 25+ Marines both in the field and classroom.
- Trained recruits in the fundamentals of marksmanship; taught classes in proper handling, maintenance, cleaning, and weapon safety.
- Experienced in use of M16A2 rifles, .45 caliber and 9mm pistols, and M500 shotguns.

Guard
- Learned all facets of apprehension techniques, including the handling of unruly personnel and crowd control.
- Worked with tactical unit and gained expertise in alarm reaction, bomb threats, terrorist and hostage reactions, and search and seizure.
- Handled vehicle and baggage searches and contacted other personnel through radio communications.
- Participated in training exercises with local police department.
- Obtained secret clearance.

**AWARDS &
HONORS**

- Prisoner Escort Qualified
- Demolitions Expert
- Rifle/Pistol Expert
- National Defense and Combat Action Ribbons
- Good Conduct Medal

**OTHER
EXPERIENCE**

VIDEO EXPRESS, Albany, NY
Manager
1992 - Present

- Oversaw entire operations of a large video entertainment retail store.
- Supervised employees and handled the overall management and security of establishment.
- Set up product and store displays to attract customers and move special merchandise.
- Performed nightly and weekly cash balancing function.
- Took regular inventory and reported to corporate headquarters on a daily and weekly basis for restocking.

**TRAVEL
EXPERIENCE**

Extensive worldwide travel, both independently and through military service; including stays in:

- France
- Switzerland
- Germany
- Portugal
- Montreal
- New England
- The Midwest
- Japan
- Spain
- Czechoslovakia
- Italy
- England
- Toronto
- California
- Florida
- South Africa

LANGUAGES

Proficient in French; presently taking courses in French and Italian.

REFERENCES

Provided upon request.

MICHAEL BEAR
P.O. Box 3515
Ann Arbor, MI 48106
(313) 761 - 0998

CAREER GOAL

To utilize strong professional and academic experience in government and political science to move into the national political arena.

PROFESSIONAL EXPERIENCE

CAMPAIGN FOR STATE REPRESENTATIVE TIMOTHY DEXTER, Ann Arbor, MI
Campaign Manager (1992 - 1993)
- Managed the successful primary and general election campaign for a first-time district candidate.
- Developed a substantial computer database of registered voters and campaign contributors and potential donors.
- Set up an extensive fundraising effort, building an extensive grassroots organization to contact voters, set up community meetings, and solicit voter participation in area events.
- Designed campaign literature and brochures and wrote and distributed press releases.
- Helped write position papers covering health insurance, economic, and other issues.

OFFICE OF STATE REPRESENTATIVE PAULA GEENA, Ann Arbor, MI
Legislative Aide (1992)
- Developed and wrote major speeches dealing with the environment, economic initiatives, and health reform.
- Wrote weekly press releases regarding voting decisions.
- Defined a program to resolve constituent issues, tracking all correspondence and telephone calls through computer database and assigning topics to interns to arrive at resolution; average turnaround reduced to four days.
- Assisted in creating internship program for area colleges and high schools.
- Participated in setting up the day to day operations of the office.

COALITION FOR PEACE, Detroit, MI
Organizer (1991)
- Coordinated membership campaign for this non-profit environmental group; built membership from 400 to 3,200 members in fifteen months.
- Hired Treasurer and worked with founder to set up board of overseers to effectively manage $120,000+ annual budget.
- Trained volunteers in methods of donation solicitation.
- Led a letter-writing campaign to members to promote participation in membership drives; realized 25% referral rate and signed on 525 additional members.

EDUCATION

UNIVERSITY OF WISCONSIN, Milwaukee, WI
Bachelor of Arts in Political Science, magna cum laude, May 1991

Activities:
- Fundraising Chairman, "Feed Your Neighbor" campaign; raised over $6,000 and collected well over 9,500 canned foods.
- President, Student Task Force to Eradicate Hunger
- Volunteer, Literacy Project

LANGUAGES

Fluency in French and English; conversant in Spanish.

ACTIVITIES

Active outdoorsman — hiking, skiing, mountain climbing, swimming; group leader in project taking school children to the wilderness to excite and develop interests in nature studies.

REFERENCES

Available upon request.

Profession: Legislative Aide   Typeface: Helvetica

NANCY SMITH
CBS Plaza, Suite 815
Sheridan, IN 46069
(317) 758 - 5027

EDUCATION

UNIVERSITY OF INDIANAPOLIS, Indianapolis, IN
Graduate School of Library & Information Science,
M.L. S., 1986

BUTLER UNIVERSITY, Indianapolis, IN
B.A., magna cum laude, 1984

LIBRARY EXPERIENCE

SHERIDAN REGIONAL LIBRARY, Sheridan, IN   1993 - Present
Librarian
- Handle the cataloging of books, music, and recordings for this research library specializing in music.
- Set up research database according to period, artist, country, and productions of published works.
- Organize all archival materials.

ANDERSON COUNTY LIBRARY ASSOCIATION, Anderson, IN   1988 - 1992
Librarian
- Ordered and cataloged new materials for this American historical reference library.
- Received and catalogued donations of historical items given by area and regional donors.
- Trained college students participating in active internship program.
- Conducted class instructions on library use and accessing journals and other historical records.
- Answered reference questions.

EVANSVILLE LIBRARY, Evansville, IN   1987
Librarian
- Supervised reference section and oversaw activities of student circulation staff.
- Set up special program for area writers and journalists to help them use research materials to develop stories, poems, fiction, and non-fiction works.

MUNCIE LIBRARY, Muncie, IN   1986
Circulation Librarian
- Checked out books, organized reserve section, and shelved books.
- Trained student assistants in cataloging and other duties.
- Handled overdue notices and fines.

OTHER EXPERIENCE

WALLACH'S, Sheridan, IN   1988 - Present
Credit Representative   (part-time, evenings)
- Consult with customers about credit accounts and initialize account process.
- Handle customer complaints and resolve account discrepancies.
- Process credit applications and bill payments.

PROFESSIONAL AFFILIATIONS

American Library Association, Member
Research Institute of America, Member
Hayden Memorial Research Society, Member & Volunteer
Sheridan Players, Member & Performer

LANGUAGES

Fluency in Spanish

Profession: Librarian   Typeface: Palatino

PARK DEEGAN
865 Broadway, #32
New York, NY 10010
(212) 673 - 5003

MUSIC BUSINESS EXPERIENCE

PRODUCER AND SONGWRITER

Produce and write songs for local band, "The Headshocks."
Arrange production of master tapes with area studios.

PRODUCER

Produced musical showcase presented in 4 area nightclubs.
Developed innovative marketing campaign with promotions director.
Worked with nightclub management to secure funding through
   ticket sales and "live participation" contests.
Negotiated special advertising and oversaw press release generation.

ASSISTANT

Helped set up and tear down indoor and outdoor sessions.
Edited and mixed various pieces.
Shipped master tapes to artists and companies around the world.

OTHER EXPERIENCE

WINDOW DESIGNER

Design special sets for clothier's large window space in the East 50's.
Change displays bi-weekly, with tie-ins to events and "memorable
   moments in history."

GRAPHIC DESIGNER

Provide individual and corporate clients with logos and brochures.

EDUCATION

Self taught, studying, on average, 70+ classics and business materials yearly.
Formal education ended with 7th grade
Took S.A.T.'s and achieved respectable scores: 670/740

OTHER DATA

Sold sitcom concept to ABC in 1987; received $70,000 rights fee.

Profession: Music Business / Designer   Typeface: Adobe Garamond

PARKER DAVIDSON

98500 Santa Monica Boulevard, #412
Los Angeles, CA 90067
(310) 553 - 0269

EDUCATION	**BERKLEE COLLEGE OF MUSIC, Boston, MA** ... Bachelor of Music Degree, December 1991 ... Major in Film Scoring
HONORS	**DEAN'S LIST** ... graduated cum laude ... Academic Excellence Certificate
MUSIC EXPERIENCE	**PROMOTER** ... for the musical group "PowerHouse" ... designed promotional kits and media releases ... developed and scheduled photo shoots ... wrote biographies of band members ... secured contracts
	ASSISTANT ... researched area markets for nightclub appearances ... compiled lists of contacts throughout industry ... helped set up calendar of events
	MANAGER ... booked events for "ENX 7" throughout San Francisco area ... prepared new releases ... handled all contracts and oversaw payroll and expenses
	PERFORMER ... performed as keyboard player for various groups performing in California, as well as Dallas and Atlanta ... received 15 month contract and bonus incentive
OTHER EXPERIENCE	**STOCKPERSON** ... organized inventory and set up special displays for The Gap's busy Newbury Street location in Boston's Back Bay ... Acted as cashier
	TELLER ... Handled individual and commercial transactions at Bank of Boston's headquarters location ... Directed customers to other services and bank products
INTERESTS	Writing, hiking, and restoring old jukeboxes

MARY JANE RIORDAN
12686 Jones Road
Houston, TX 77070
(713) 890 - 4689

OBJECTIVE

To use 7 years of proven nursing, teaching, and writing experience to develop programs in a hospital or day care setting which focus on children's needs.

PROFESSIONAL EXPERIENCE

MEMORIAL CITY MEDICAL CENTER, Houston, TX   4/89 - Present
Coordinator (4/90 - Present)
- Handle staff scheduling for daily assignments for a 60 bed unit.
- Perform quarterly and yearly evaluations of personnel.
- Participate in the primary care decision making process, dealing with all levels of staff and families of patients.

Registered Nurse (4/89 - 3/90)
- Performed assignments in both staff and charge positions on various shifts and throughout all wards.

METHODIST HOSPITAL, Houston, TX   3/88 - 3/89
Registered Nurse
- Worked in a 32 bed rehabilitation unit, with responsibilities for assisting in daily rehab management.
- Developed an aggressive family and patient education program to train family members in patient care activities.

TEXAS CHILDREN'S HOSPITAL, Houston, TX   5/86 - 2/88
Ward Coordinator
- Trained all new personnel in ward procedures.
- Oversaw Medicare and Medicaid processing requirements.
- Taught classes for families and patients on many various issues facing those who are terminally ill.

PUBLICATIONS

"What's the Matter with Mommy"
A 24-page story about a mother who is terminally ill and how to help the children affected; story bought by Sentry Publishers and will be distributed nationwide in November, 1993, with an initial 30,000 printing.

COMMUNITY ACTIVITIES

HOUSTON BAPTIST UNIVERSITY, Houston, TX   Winter 1993
Speaker
- Speak to community groups on how to create programs dealing with the terminally ill.
- Meet with government and agency officials to set community approaches to health care.

FARNSWORTH SCHOOL, Houston, TX   1987 - 1990
Teacher
- Worked with children of terminally ill parents to develop ways to deal with issues of loss, abandonment, and survival.
- Conducted weekly sessions for groups of parents to define the family unit in relation to family loss.

LANGUAGES

Fluent in Spanish.

EDUCATION

RICE UNIVERSITY, Houston, TX
BSN In Nursing, December 1985

BOSTON UNIVERSITY, Boston, MA
Undergraduate studies in Public Relations
September 1982 - May 1983

REFERENCES

Available upon request.

STEVEN GOULD
212 North Pleasant Street
Amherst, MA 01004
(413) 549 - 1182

OBJECTIVE   To utilize proven experience in nursing to contribute in
a critical care environment.

**WORK
EXPERIENCE**   **AMHERST HOSPITAL**, Amherst, MA   **1991 - Present**
Critical Care Nurse — Intensive Care Unit

- Provide primary nursing care for up to three critically ill
  patients suffering from varied types of trauma.
- Handle the management of patients, including invasive
  central lines, cardiac monitors, and respirators.
- Follow prescribed medical procedures to restore stability,
  prevent complications, and attain patient health.

BOSTON CITY HOSPITAL, Boston, MA   **1988 - 1991**
Critical Care Nurse — Trauma Unit

- Provided primary nursing care for one or two critically ill
  patients in a nine bed trauma unit.
- Acted as charge nurse while staff member was on leave;
  coordinated unit activities and worked with patients and
  their families and instructed them on all levels of care.

BETH ISRAEL HOSPITAL, Boston, MA   **1986 - 1988**
Staff Nurse

- For pre- and post-operative cardiac patients, monitored
  telemetries recording and documenting arrhythmias.

FAULKNER HOSPITAL, Boston, MA   **1985**
Staff Nurse

EDUCATION   **NORTHEASTERN UNIVERSITY**, Boston, MA
Bachelor of Science in Nursing, magna cum laude, 1985

LICENSES   Massachusetts and Rhode Island State Nursing Licenses

CERTIFICATES   CCRN Certified
Advance Life Support Certification
American Association of Critical Care Nurses

REFERENCES   Provided upon request.

STAN McDONALD
134 Wright Brothers Drive, #6
Salt Lake City, UT 84116
(801) 575 - 2885

PROFESSIONAL OBJECTIVE

To use proven management expertise in Facilities/Operations Management to contribute to a leading and expanding corporation.

SUMMARIZED QUALIFICATIONS

- Expertise in communications, public relations, negotiations, and staff training and development.
- Ability to cultivate professional attitude among employees while streamlining existing systems and operations.
- Overseeing project coordination, communications, and staff planning.
- Troubleshooting and developing operational controls to maximize profits.

PROFESSIONAL EXPERIENCE

PROVO/SALT LAKE ENTERPRISES, Salt Lake City, UT   1987 - Present
Site Manager

- Supervise staff of 52, managing a $2.4 million budget, with overall responsibility for payroll, benefits administration, and operating expenses.
- Direct the production of 2.6 million copies per month for law firms using reprographics services.
- Act as primary liaison between internal staff and over 500 corporate end users.

BRENNAN, SMITH, JOHNSON & SMYTHE, New York, NY   1983 - 1987
Facilities Director

- Managed two supervisors and nine permanent staff in a law firm's copy center servicing over 95 attorneys and 260 total staff.
- Streamlined operations and cut overall expenses by $62,000 within eight months.
- Set up ordering system to reduce inventories while maintaining smooth operations.

PROVO RESORT, Provo, UT   1978 - 1983
Division Executive

- Managed 5 department heads and over 100 employees. Set agenda for enhancing revenues, ensuring budget compliance, developing growth strategies, and streamlining operations.
- Handled the complete operations of the facility during General Manager's six month absence. Maintained profit/loss responsibility for Rooms Division, including Rooms, Engineering, Security, Housekeeping, Front Office, and Reservations departments.
- Initiated a corporate development program to build effective working relationships between divisions.

EDUCATION

WAGNER COLLEGE, Staten Island, NY
Bachelor of Science degree in Business Administration, magna cum laude, 1977

Profession: Operations Management   Typeface: Adobe Garamond

NANCY SCHIFERSE

47 Bristol Court Lane
Damariscotta, ME
04543
(207) 563 - 1715

Typeface: Adobe Garamond

Profession: Photographer

EDUCATION

1993	**PARSONS SCHOOL OF DESIGN**, New York, NY *B.F.A. Photography*, with concentrated coursework in Realism
Summer 1992	**JACK CENTAUR**, School of Photography, Boston, MA — Private Study
Summer 1991	**EASTMAN KODAK CENTER**, Camden, ME Winter Program; Studies in Photography and Computer Imaging

RELATED EXPERIENCE

Summer 1992	**BACK BAY NEWS**, Boston, MA *Freelance Photographer* — Took photographs of people and places around the city of Boston. Published 11 photographs over 8-month time period. Won 1st place award in Boston Photo Competition '91 for photograph of architectural montage of city.
Summer 1991	**AGFA DESIGN GROUP**, Waterville, ME *Intern* — Assisted senior computer imaging consultant with annual report for 3 regional companies. Researched stock images and helped scan images into Macintosh FX computer.
Summer 1990	**DAVID WRIGHT**, Boston, MA & Portland, ME *Intern* — Performed various darkroom and office tasks for an independent photographer.

OTHER EXPERIENCE

Summer 1992	**FRED'S WATERING HOLE**, Marblehead, MA Bartender
Summer 1991	**STOCK & GARAGE**, Camden, ME Waitress
Summer 1989	**THE GAP**, Boston, MA Stockperson

REFERENCES
AVAILABLE UPON REQUEST

D A R L A   J O H N S T O N

123 Commerce Street • East Haven, CT
0 6 5 1 2

(203) 468 - 8211

PROFESSIONAL EXPERIENCE

CAMDEN HART STUDIOS, East Haven, CT   10/90 - Present
Photography Studio Coordinator

- Scouted, organized, and coordinated locations in the United States, Canada, Europe, and Africa.
- Set up aggressive marketing campaign which doubled client base.
- Negotiated contracts with individual and corporate clients.
- Oversaw legal rights to copyrights, trademarks, and use fees.
- Researched the development of a house catalogue; developed a comprehensive stock listing sent to over 400 corporate accounts, raising revenues by 45%.

JACOB BRENNAN, New York, NY   3/87 - 8/90
Stock Manager

- Catalogued the inventory of a stock house with over 200,000 photographs.
- Prepared portfolios used by photographers on sales calls to advertising agencies and corporate accounts.
- Implemented media campaign using press releases, brochures, and sample kits, resulting in 40 new accounts as well as 8 articles written for industry publications.

PROVIDENCE PHOTOGRAPHY COLLABORATIVE, Providence, RI   4/83 - 1/87
Exhibition Planner

- Installed photography shows on a 3-week rotating basis representing classic and contemporary works.
- Created wall descriptions, artist's statement sheet, and price lists for potential clients and media use.
- Organized receptions and special tie-ins with seasonal events.
- Documented, insured, and shipped artworks for traveling shows.

EDUCATION

SCHOOL OF THE MUSEUM OF FINE ARTS, Boston, MA
Bachelor of Fine Arts, May 1982
Concentrations in Photography and Art History

Relevant Coursework:
- ▼ Fundamentals of Black & White Design
- ▼ Lighting I, II, and III
- ▼ Urban Design in Architectural Photography
- ▼ Digital Imaging
- ▼ Nature Photography
- ▼ Consumer Products

INTERNSHIP

BAXTER PHOTOGRAPHY, Boston, MA
Gallery Assistant
- Helped set up shows.
- Worked with artists to matte and frame photographs.

LANGUAGES

Proficiency in German; limited reading comprehension in French.

REFERENCES

Professional references and samples of marketing material available upon request.

Profession: Photographer's Assistant   Typeface: Avant Garde

Typeface: Helvetica

Profession: Photography Assistant

JOSHUA PIXTON
7109 Dayton Pike
Hixson, TN 37343
(615) 842 - 0663

OBJECTIVE   To build upon proven experience in New York studios as a photographer's assistant and contribute to the projects of a nature photographer.

EDUCATION   **BARNARD COLLEGE**, New York, NY
Bachelor of Arts in English, December 1992
Minor in Photography

Photography Coursework:
- Studio Photography
- Advanced B&W Printing
- Color Printing
- Studio Lighting

SCHOOL OF VISUAL ARTS, New York, NY
6-month Intensive Photography Program

PHOTOGRAPHY EXPERIENCE   <u>*Worked as an assistant to the following in New York City:*</u>

PIERRE CENTAUR
Fashion Photographer

JACQUES MALCORPS
Still Life Photographer

BARBARA KAUFMANN
Still Life Photographer

ARNOLD KLEMP
Fashion Photographer

OTHER EXPERIENCE   **CAMP STILWATER**, Stilwater, NY
Camp Counselor
- Planned summer playground site and conducted subsequent weekly safety inspections.
- Counseled 22+ children ranging in age from six to ten years.

TAYLOR RECYCLING PLANT, Utica, NY
Assistant
- Recycled plastics and repaired processing equipment.
- Assisted in the installation of new systems.

SKILLS   Excellent office skills — handling correspondence, typing, answering telephones, filing, and researching materials.

LANGUAGES   General knowledge of French and Spanish.

REFERENCES   Excellent letters of recommendation available upon request.

GLORIA MEEHAN
1864 W. 4th Street
Tempe, AZ 85281
(602) 350 - 2178

EDUCATION   **BOSTON UNIVERSITY**, Boston, MA   December 1992
MBA

COLUMBIA UNIVERSITY, New York, NY   May 1990
BSBA in Finance, with Honors
Dean's List

Activities:
Co-Chair — "Project Promise," fundraising event for special needs
students from area elementary schools to create linkage program between
undergraduate students and special needs classes.

WORK
EXPERIENCE   **U.S. TRUST COMPANY**, Boston, MA   Fall 1991 - Spring 1993
Project Analyst

- Analyzed market share of Fortune 500 companies, with emphasis on
  channels of distribution and abilities to maximize efficiencies.
- Presented weekly written reports to senior management team and
  made oral presentations with suggestions for streamlining project.
- Conducted extensive study into international trade relations on a
  variety of products. Analyzed influences of trade competition,
  government restrictions, tariffs, and other issues affecting imports
  and exports.
- Worked with liquor industry executives to formulate an approach
  to enter U.S. and Canadian markets. Set up computerized database
  to track findings relating to 100+ suppliers, dozens of shippers,
  government regulatory bodies, retail markets, and others. Maintained
  factual details on over 800 sources.

CHEMICAL BANK, New York, NY   Winter 1990 - Fall 1991
Analyst

- Prepared reports to strengthen strategic decisions affecting a chain
  of dry cleaning establishments (65 businesses located throughout 5 states).
- Established criteria for expansion, setting aggressive schedules to open
  an additional 110 businesses over a three year time frame.
- Prepared monthly income statements, balance sheets, cash flow analyses,
  and tracking reports on personnel growth and related cost containment
  for a biomedical firm.

MANUFACTURERS HANOVER, New York, NY   Summer 1989
Administrative Assistant

- Assisted 3 managers with their portfolios and related transactions.

COMPUTER
SKILLS   Solid understanding of WordPerfect and Lotus 1-2-3 applications.

LANGUAGES   Fluent in German and Spanish; conversational abilities in French.

INTERESTS   Extensive travel throughout the United States, Europe, and Africa.

Profession: Portfolio Analyst / Banking   Typeface: Times

JANET BLANKS
121 Summer Street
Stamford, CT 06901
(203) 348 - 3365

**SUMMARY
OF STRENGTHS**

❏ Proven ability to achieve agency goals while providing optimal care
to adolescents and adults at risk.

❏ Successful administrative experience, setting up agency, family, and
patient schedules and appointments to fulfill all program goals.

❏ Experienced team leader, organizing events and coordinating all
related activities to ensure successful development of participant goals.

**PROFESSIONAL
EXPERIENCE**

CONNECTICUT STATE PRISON, New Haven, CT   **1992 - Present**
Program Coordinator
- Act as community liaison with community based educational systems,
court systems, local clinics, caseworkers, and families of youth
participating in program.
- Provide outreach support services to adolescents who are transitioning
from secure treatment facilities into their communities.
- Assist youth with their transition agenda and promote a stable and
rewarding environment.
- Participate in overseeing caseworkers and clinical staff.

AUGUSTA CORRECTIONAL FACILITY, Augusta, ME   **1987 - 1992**
Program Coordinator
- Implemented group and recreational activities for at risk adolescents
with responsibilities for interviewing program participants and developing
programs that stimulate skills and educational development.
- Directed all contact with juvenile court probation officers and social
services liaisons.
- Set up outreach services for caseworkers, clients, and client families.
- Oversaw activities of caseworkers and clinical staff.

PORTLAND JUVENILE DETENTION CENTER, Portland, ME   **1986 - 1987**
Program Supervisor
- Assisted Director in the administration of case management and staff
supervision.
- Coordinated client referrals and assisted staff in assessment and
treatment of clients.
- Provided crisis intervention and developed outside resources for clients.
- Built modules to monitor participant safety and security procedures.

PORTLAND DAY CENTER, Portland, ME   **1985**
Probation Officer
- Monitored client behavior, conducted security checks, and provided
crisis intervention.
- Utilized physical restraint techniques as necessary.

EDUCATION

MAINE STATE COLLEGE, Augusta, ME
Bachelor of Science in Criminal Justice, May 1985

Internship:

BRUNSWICK CORRECTIONAL FACILITY, Brunswick, ME   **Fall/Winter 1984**
Probation Aide Intern
- Researched case histories in juvenile court setting.
- Learned court procedures through daily session observation.

LANGUAGES

One year adult education program in Spanish; registered for one year
intensive program in Spanish language, with emphasis on developing
verbal skills.

REFERENCES   Provided upon request.

C. JOSEPH EMORY
2900 S.W. Dolph Court, Unit 4
Portland, OR 97219
(503) 245 - 9406

AREAS OF
EXPERTISE

Hardware:

IBM 3090, IBM PC XT, IBM 4381, IBM 3083, Honeywell 66/DPS3, VAX 780, and VAX 8600.

Languages:

Expertise in SAS, CSP, RPG, PL/1, and COBOL

Software:

DB2/SQL, IMS/DLI, CICS, OS/JCL, VSAM, MVS/XA, DOS, TSO/ISPF, and numerous word processing, spreadsheet, and graphic applications.

PROFESSIONAL
EXPERIENCE

XITEC SYSTEMS, Portland, OR   **1/91 - Present**
Programming Manager

- Develop systems used for insurance claims processing, including the analysis and development of user specifications, coding new programs, testing, and implementation for production use.
- Design emergency back-up procedures and 24-hour on call support.
- Use COBOL, SAS, DB2/SQL, IMS/DLI, VSAM, and OS/JCL in an IBM environment.
- Create extensive programming and user documentation libraries.

JCM TECHNICAL DATA FORMS, Hillsboro, OR   **7/87 - 12/90**
Programmer

- Led programming efforts for the claims division, with major responsibilities for batch processing enhancements, designing on-line input for processing clerks, and creating manuals for end users.
- Use COBOL, IMS/DL1, CICS, OS/JCL, VSAM, AND RPG in an IBM environment.

PARKER KNOWLEDGE SYSTEMS, Eugene, OR   **6/86 - 6/87**
Analyst

- Wrote programs for a cost analysis system used by senior management to assess divisional performance.
- Enabled division managers to streamline processing, reduce staff by 10%, and cut expenses by 18% within one year.

PCC DESIGNS, Corvallis, OR   **6/84 - 6/86**
Programmer
- Designed batch control and tracking procedures for a retailer with over 500 suppliers.
- Cut inventory control costs by 40%.
- Identified slow moving items and eliminated excessive or duplicate ordering.

LANGUAGES   Fluent in German; Reading comprehension of Italian.

EDUCATION   **PORTLAND UNIVERSITY**, Portland, OR
                     Bachelor of Arts in Computer Science, May 1984

REFERENCES   Furnished upon request.

Profession: Programmer   Typeface: Helvetica

PARKER LOLLING
319 Silverside Avenue
Little Silver, NJ 07739
(201) 842 - 1893

EDUCATION

EMERSON COLLEGE, Boston, MA
Bachelor of Science in Communications, December 1990
Dean's List
Activities:
❑ Founder and Treasurer, College Promotions Group
❑ Member, Intercultural Association

RELEVANT HISTORY

STEPHEN LOLLING PROMOTIONS, Middletown, NJ   **1/92 - Present**
Promotions Director (9/92 - Present)
• Collaborated with area promoters to arrange successful concert program.
• Initiated and launched sales division to obtain exclusive arrangements with area businesses.
• Planned and directed annual benefit event.

Promotions Assistant (1/92 - 8/92)
• Wrote on-air promotions and giveaways for radio personalities.
• Coordinated promotions and set up call-in agendas.

J & J ENTERPRISES, Atlantic City, NJ   **6/91 - 12/91**
Promotions Assistant
• Assisted in creating and distributing press releases to area media.
• Hosted album release parties and set up contacts to maximize promotions strategies.

INGALLS, QUINN & JOHNSON, Boston, MA   **12/90 - 5/91**
Assistant
• Helped director choose talent and verified applicant credentials.
• Answered all correspondence and reviewed materials with Director weekly.

LESLEY PRODUCTIONS, Boston, MA   **Fall 1989**
Intern
• Worked with staff to set up concert and party promotions.
• Participated in designing flyers for upcoming events.
• Proofed copy and submitted materials to local media.

OTHER WORK EXPERIENCE

JACK'S, Boston, MA   **Fall/Winter 1989**
Disc Jockey
• Initiated and hosted alternative music night, parts of which were telecast live on area college radio station.

ANN TAYLOR, Boston, MA   **Part-Time 1988**
Associate
• Monitored cash inflow/outflow and summarized sales and profit figures on a daily basis.
• Submitted weekly reports to management.

SYSTEM SKILLS

❑ IBM, using Lotus 1-2-3 and WordPerfect
❑ Macintosh, using Microsoft Word

LANGUAGES

Proficient in Italian.

JOHN BORGES

68 Kellers Farm Road
Easton, CT 06612
(203) 459 - 6651

EDUCATION

RUTGERS, Newark, NJ
Bachelor of Arts in Economics, May 1992
Dean's List

WORK HISTORY

WILLIAM BORGES PRODUCTIONS, Easton, CT   6/92 - Present
Promotions Assistant
- Work within the promotions division conducting survey analyses, telephone promotions, and research of industry trends.
- Assist in organizing tour details for major acts scheduled to appear in the United States and throughout Europe.
- Contact tour locations to verify that all aspects of tour are on schedule.
- Help create special mailers and billboard designs to generate maximum sales.
- Write press releases for all media.

NEW YORK INNER CITY NETWORK, New York, NY   Summer 1991
Researcher
- Collected data on inner city conditions of childhood, with particular focus on certain New York neighborhoods.
- Helped set up roundtable conferences to discuss collected data and suggest ways for social and political reforms to be enacted in order to solve problems.
- Authored an in-depth report on the effect of lone parent families and a child's success socially and in the education process.

SKILLS

- Over 6 years of performing with local orchestras, jazz bands, and in various nightclubs.
- Highly athletic, with experience in a wide range of activities; willingness to participate in any sports activity with clients.
- Strong writing abilities, with proven experience in technical writing, developing grant proposals, and writing press releases.

LANGUAGES

General verbal competency in Spanish and Portuguese.

REFERENCES

Available upon request.

EVELYN PURDY
55 Belview Drive
Natick, MA 01760
(508) 653 - 5128

CAREER OBJECTIVES

▲ To utilize proven academic strength and internship experience to contribute to a results-driven organization.
▲ To participate in the creative stages and management of a product launch.
▲ Becoming recognized as a industry leader, sought for knowledge and expertise in the public relations field.

EDUCATION

EMERSON COLLEGE, Boston, MA
Bachelor of Arts in Mass Communications, May 1993

Coursework:
• Public Relations
• Advertising
• Public Opinion and Behavioral Analysis
• Oral Presentations

INTERNSHIP EXPERIENCE

INGALLS, QUINN & JOHNSON, Boston, MA   **Fall 1992**
Intern

• Coordinated presentations for corporate business meetings.
• Prepared press releases for production launches and participated as a public relations assistant.
• Translated various documents from French and Italian to English.
• Participated in the development of an ad campaign for Reebok.
• Organized the division's visual files, including materials on sports equipment, athletic clothing, healthcare products, wines, soft drinks, and miscellaneous other products.
• Set up spreadsheet applications with Microsoft Excel on the Macintosh.
• Designed 12 different templates using Microsoft Word for generating proposals.

HARPER FERRY COMPANY, Boston, MA   **Spring 1992**
Intern

• Maintained and organized financial documents and transcripts.
• Met with clients and compiled information for them on project status.
• Contributed new ideas to project managers; received recognition for having one idea become major concept for ad campaign.

WHEELOCK & GARBER ASSOCIATES, Cambridge, MA   **Fall 1991**
Intern

• Conducted interviews at various malls throughout the region to determine product viability.
• Filled out comprehensive analysis reports to reflect consumer reaction to four different products.
• Presented findings to management committee on a weekly basis.

ACTIVITIES

▲ Member, Public Relations Society of America
▲ Member & Volunteer, Somalia Global Relief Effort
▲ Member & Volunteer Researcher, Amnesty International
▲ Extensive travel throughout the United States, Europe, and Africa

LANGUAGES

Fluent in French, Spanish, and Italian; conversant in German.

REFERENCES

Available upon request.

MARTHA WOLDMAN
99 Chapel Street, #5
Portsmouth, NH 03801
(603) 431 - 2674

**PROFESSIONAL
EXPERIENCE**
NORTHERN LIGHTS, Portsmouth, NH   **1989 - Present**
Marketing Coordinator

- Handle the seasonal marketing plans for between 20 and 25 newly published books, primarily non-fiction works.
- Act as liaison between the sales, marketing, and fulfillment divisions.
- Manage an annual marketing budget of $220,000+.
- Approve media campaigns, write press releases, and coordinate the direct mail efforts focused on the book trade and to selected professional audiences.
- Prepare layout, brochures, and giveaways for annual conventions.
- Work with sales force to promote titles and market selected titles according to seasonal demands and reviews.
- Meet with senior management team on a quarterly basis to report on projections versus realized sales, new developments with writers, and market analyses and their use in strategizing media and market coverage.
- Participate in the production of company newsletter, with responsibility for writing a quarterly feature related to marketing and publishing.

GANNETT GROUP, New York, NY   **1985 - 1989**
Direct Mail/Catalog Coordinator

- Set up extensive database to include retail accounts, wholesalers, individuals, and media sources (editors, reviewers, producers, and others) to generate maximum exposure for titles and authors. Achieved 8,300 reliable names and addresses within one year period.
- Supervised the planning efforts for regional trade shows, the American Booksellers Association's annual convention, the American Library Association's convention, and other events.
- Developed special promotions for public events; realized a 60% recall rate amongst show participants and received overall praise for innovative promotions.

BERKELEY & BIDDLE, Boston, MA   **1983 - 1984**
Proofreader/Administrative Assistant

- Proofread quarterly and seasonal catalogs sent to industry and individual clients.
- Reviewed all sales materials to verify accuracy of factual data, such as names and addresses, prices noted, descriptions properly given, etc.
- Worked with designers to put together catalogs and brochures.

SEMINARS
- Pre-press Strategies with the Macintosh
- Copywriting
- Countdown 2000 — Interactive Media
- Direct Mail — Strategies for the 90s
- Effective Listening

EDUCATION
UNIVERSITY OF NEW HAMPSHIRE, Durham, NH
Bachelor of Arts in English, May 1983

LANGUAGES
Proficient in Italian and Spanish.

REFERENCES
Available upon request.

Profession: Publishing / Marketing   Typeface: Avant Garde

Profession: Radio Announcer / Writer   *Typeface: Adobe Garamond*

ROBERT C. PRICKETT

701 Adams Avenue
Memphis, TN 38105
(901) 527 - 1818

OBJECTIVE

To develop skills in radio by contributing experience to an entry level on-air position.

EDUCATION

UNIVERSITY OF SOUTHERN CALIFORNIA,
Los Angeles, CA
Certificate in Radio and Television Broadcasting, 1993
Certificate in Live Performance, 1992

INTERNSHIPS

NASHVILLE SPORTS ARENA, Nashville, TN
Public Address Announcer
Spring 1993

NEW YORK HISPANIC DAILY, New York, NY
Reporter
Spring 1992

RELATED SKILLS

Play by Play Announcing
Voice-overs
Color Analyst
Sports and News Writing
Copywriting

COMPUTER SKILLS

Three years experience using Macintosh computer and various software applications.

LANGUAGES

Fluent in Spanish.

ACTIVITIES

Active volunteer in various programs related to the Spanish community; using experience as a volunteer to the New York Spanish Coalition to develop programs in Tennessee school systems.

OTHER DATA

Willing to relocate for short or long term assignments.

REFERENCES

References and tapes available upon request.

DOUGLAS R. GONLEY
4010 Commercial Avenue
Northbrook, IL 60062
(708) 205 - 1488

SUMMARY OF STRENGTHS

- Over eight years proven success negotiating and selling real estate deals and packages.
- Extensive experience building relationships with developers, lenders, and clients.
- Expertise in commercial, residential, and new construction projects, with career sales totaling over $40 million.

WORK EXPERIENCE

1989 - Present

EXECUTIVE REALTY MANAGEMENT, Northbrook, IL
Sales Executive
- Sold luxury condominiums and commercial properties, maintaining #1 position in company during down market cycle.
- Oversaw staff of seven realtors and support staff.
- Helped developers through the permit and conversion process for 120-unit condominium development; realized a 100% sell out within eight months.
- Structured tax shelter deals for investors.

1988

CHICAGO LIVING PARTNERS, De Kalb, IL
Sales Director
- Promoted shared living development and sold 80 units (80% of development) during pre-construction phase.
- Met with advisory board to plan for activity spaces such as exercise area, tennis courts, child care rooms, and performance stage.
- Developed client profile analysis to target prospects through specific media sources. Prepared market surveys.
- Reached 100% occupancy within six months after construction.

1984 - 1987

KELLER DEVELOPMENTS, Chicago, IL
Coordinator
- Hired management staff to operate 85 unit condominium development.
- Negotiated contracts with service professionals to care for common areas, grounds, and building maintenance.
- Established written procedures for maintenance, raising standards while reducing costs by 12% in 1985 and 8% in 1986.
- Set up innovative advertising campaigns, increasing traffic by 30% over previous methods used.

1983

INDEPENDENT TRAVEL, Paris, France
Various Assignments
- Traveled extensively throughout Europe with primary residence in Paris.
- Spent 15 months exploring the arts and cultures of European communities.
- Wrote travel and art-related pieces for U.S. newspapers.
- Supported living expenses through fashion modeling and house-sitting.

EDUCATION

1982

UNIVERSITY OF CHICAGO, Chicago, IL
Undergraduate studies in Business Administration

LANGUAGES

Proficiency in French, Spanish, and Italian.

REFERENCES

Furnished upon request.

Profession: Realtor   Typeface: Helvetica

Typeface: Helvetica

Profession: Realtor / Property Management

JOHN LAWSON
100 Main Street
Yorktown, VA 23690
(804) 887 - 2874

QUALIFICATIONS

- Results oriented real estate professional with extensive experience in sales and property management.
- Successful track record in creating and implementing effective marketing strategies to sell developed properties.
- Proven ability to resolve issues with contractors, public agencies, and private groups.
- Excellent communication skills, with outstanding ability to cultivate and maintain long term relationships with industry professionals.

PROFESSIONAL EXPERIENCE

WASHINGTON DEVELOPMENT GROUP, Richmond, VA   **1987 - Present**
Commercial Developments/Leasing Agent
- Sell and promote shopping centers, apartment complexes, and vacant land for retail development.
- Negotiate and close leases with tenants.
- Meet with property owners and developers to gain exclusive rights to market properties.
- Work as liaison between banks, investors, and property owners to package construction and permanent financing.
- Negotiate for advertising space in local and regional media.
- Provide copy for advertisements.

ALEXANDRIA INVESTMENT PARTNERS, Alexandria, VA   **1984 - 1987**
Investment/Retail Leasing Broker
- Marketed and sold apartment complexes, shopping centers, and land for retail development.
- Represented developers and owners in the marketing and promotion campaigns for new commercial developments.
- Obtain exclusive leasing rights for luxury units in Washington, D.C. area.
- Developed sales campaigns and closed deals through the placing of financing for buyers.
- Worked with consultant to create a computerized lease tracking system.
- Wrote press releases.

NORFOLK PROPERTIES, Norfolk, VA   **1975 - 1984**
Property Manager (1978 - 1984)
- Scheduled and supervised all interior, exterior, and mechanical maintenance for over 150 units in 11 area properties.
- Solicited and received work quotes; coordinated resulting job construction.
- Supervised any construction build-outs and represented interests of owners in tenant negotiations.
- Negotiated leases with tenants.
- Advertised developments through print, radio, and special promotions.

Maintenance Superintendent (1975 - 1978)
- Maintained hands on supervision of 30 unit condominium building, with overall responsibility for security, repairs, contractor and tenant relations, emergency response, and code enforcements.

COMPUTERS   Proficiency with IBM and Macintosh computers; familiarity with various software.

EDUCATION   **NORFOLK STATE UNIVERSITY**, Norfolk, VA
Bachelor of Science in Marketing, May 1983
Honors:
- Graduated cum laude
- National Honor Society
- Dean's List, six of eight semesters

STELLA KAGAN
48 Central Avenue
Lexington, KY 40502
(606) 253 - 6518

RELEVANT EXPERIENCE

LEXINGTON GROUP NEWS INC., Lexington, KY
Reporter
- Investigate events, perform extensive research, and write news and feature articles based on area and regional people and events.

GANETT NEWSPAPERS, Louisville, KY
Reporter
- Hired to write freelance articles which covered crime and health issues.

DAILY REPORTER, Cincinnati, OH
Writer's Assistant
- Supported reporters in the preparation of their stories; gathered materials, researched leads, and wrote rough outlines for their review and revision.
- Reviewed press releases to determine potential news leads.

EDUCATION

SPALDING UNIVERSITY, Louisville, NY
Bachelor of Arts in English, May 1992
Minor in Newswriting

Work Study Program:

Career Assistant — Career Planning & Placement Office
- Trained and supervised all volunteers over an eight month period.
- Edited bi-weekly newsletter sent to all recent graduates.
- Contacted employers to solicit job leads for undergraduate internship program.

INTERNSHIP

OFFICE OF STATE REPRESENTATIVE JOHN "JOCK" HARRIMAN, Washington, DC
Senior Intern, Fall 1991
- Participated in the organization of monthly workshops for first-time interns.
- Organized, scheduled, and conducted Capitol tours.
- Corresponded with constituents and resolved issues under staff supervision.

Intern, Fall 1990
- Learned a wide range of responsibilities to support activities of representative.
- Recorded all correspondence and helped perform research to answer requests.

POST GRADUATION ACTIVITIES
- Participant in college's Model United Nations
- Active volunteer in Democratic political campaign events
- Member and Volunteer to Amnesty International
- Graduate level courses in Writing Non-Fiction and Researching Corporations

LANGUAGES   Bilingual in English and Spanish.

AFFILIATIONS   News Writers of New York, 2 years

REFERENCES   Available upon request.

Profession: Reporter / Writer   Typeface: Palatino

PETER SCHOELKOPF

5821 Doyle Street • Emeryville, CA 94608 • (510) 523 - 7842

PROFESSIONAL OBJECTIVE

To obtain a position where successful work performance, effective interpersonal skills, and supervisory leadership will contribute to the achievement of an organization's goals.

SUMMARY OF STRENGTHS

Over thirteen years of restaurant experience with proven abilities in management, problem-solving, customer relations, planning and organization, and marketing.

ACCOMPLISHMENTS

- Chosen by corporate headquarters to lead business seminars for new supervisors and operations personnel.
- Led development of in-house banquet facility with a 22% realized increase in gross revenues.
- Received three promotions over a five year period, with current responsibility for 35 staff and gross revenues of over $2.6 million.
- Initiate innovative promotional campaigns to cater to area students and young professionals; received free media attention from 2 television networks.
- Developed database to track revenue across all product lines and create monthly reports used for strategic planning.

PROFESSIONAL HISTORY

SHERATON RESTAURANT GROUP   1989 - Present
San José, CA

- Manage all operations, including restaurant, bar, and entertainment lounge with annual revenues over $2.6 million.

SAN FRANCISCO GUEST SUITES   1987 - 1988
San Francisco, CA

- Handled responsibilities for all restaurant operations.

PARKER'S   1982 - 1986
San Francisco, CA

- Built banquet facilities which contributed 40% to revenues within one year.

COASTAL PARTNERS, INC.   1979 - 1981
Santa Cruz, CA

- Supervised wait staff, with responsibility for training all new personnel.

LANGUAGES

General knowledge of Spanish and Italian.

PERSONAL

Willingness to relocate.

HARRY MANSFIELD
807 Jefferson Hwy
Baton Rouge, LA 70806
(504) 927 - 0682

EDUCATION

BACHELOR OF SCIENCE IN FOOD MANAGEMENT   1987
Loyola University, New Orleans, LA

Related Coursework:
- Managing Food Service Personnel
- Dining Room Service
- Accounting Principles I & II
- Food Quantities and Production
- Cost Accounting
- Liability in the Workplace

CERTIFICATIONS

Hospitality and Restaurant Management - American Restaurant Association
Food Service Sanitation - National Hotel Association
Emergency First Aid - American Red Cross

**PROVEN
SKILLS**

PLANNING AND PRODUCTION
- Projecting volumes and traffic flows for proposed locations
- Identifying proper space allowances based on daily clientele, menu, and employees in kitchen and serving areas
- Developing proper menus for selected regions

EMPLOYEE TRAINING
- Creating training modules defining daily work assignments and measuring performance
- Verifying compliance with quality control standards
- Teaching all staff alternate skills to back-up other areas during busy periods

FOOD COSTING
- Determining menu prices according to profit ratio requirements
- Varying recipes to raise yields per item
- Providing kitchen staff with written standards for portion control

**PROFESSIONAL
EXPERIENCE**

Natchez Enterprises, Baton Rouge, LA   1992 - Present
Night Manager
- Increased weekend sales by 32% through special promotions and displays which raised average party size from 3 to 5 people.
- Lowered spoilage dramatically with smaller, more frequent ordering and maintaining proper portion controls.
- Supervised staff of 26, including 2 shift supervisors for establishment seating 350.
- Established weekly staff meetings to set ensure compliance with quality standards.
- Successfully met increased weekend sales with no additional staff.
- Initiated Saturday afternoon buffet

Billy's, Bossier City, LA   1988 - 1991
Kitchen Supervisor
- Managed all kitchen operations for a large restaurant emphasizing family fare and special family promotions.
- Planned and priced nightly specials on a weekly basis.
- Provided ad copy to general manager for weekend advertising promotions.
- Set up quality control program which was adopted by 3 other affiliated companies.

**COMPUTER
SKILLS**

Lotus 1-2-3, WordPerfect 5.1, Microsoft Excel

REFERENCES

Available upon request.

Profession: Restaurant Manager   Typeface: Palatino

MATT FLEMING
14 West St. George Boulevard
Apartment 14
St. George, UT 84770

OBJECTIVE	To utilize over 7 years of proven experience and abilities in the food service industry to obtain a challenging and growth-oriented position.

EDUCATION

LAYTON COLLEGE, Layton, UT
Bachelor of Science in Food Management, May 1985
Dean's List, 3 semesters

Relevant Coursework:
- Restaurant Management
- Food Quality in Regional Foods
- Principles of Restaurant Operations
- Financial Statements
- Taxation Principles

RELEVANT EXPERIENCE

UNIVERSITY GRILLS, St. George, UT   **4/88 - Present**
Manager
- Handle all management responsibilities for 35 staff, including front and back operations for this fine dining establishment.
- Perform hiring, training, and scheduling duties for all shifts.
- Work with accountant to process weekly payroll and submit tax payments.
- Manage a yearly, extensive 2 week training program for supervisors, with hands on training exercises and development of new skills.
- Maintain computer database for weekly food and liquor inventory.
- Project cyclical variables and design special promotional events to sustain and increase cash flow.

RICK'S, St. George, UT   **6/86 - 2/88**
Assistant Manager
- Ordered food and liquor inventory on a daily and weekly basis.
- Scheduled employees to maximize efficiencies for extremely busy early morning shifts and late afternoon dinner specials.
- Designed advertising for area newspapers; provided copy and artwork.

CHIKA CHAKA, Provo, UT   **6/85 - 5/86**
Supervisor
- Worked over 20 hours per week throughout undergraduate term, with 50+ hour work weeks during summers and school breaks.
- Worked with architects and designers during renovations of restaurant.
- Created logo used on all letterheads, advertisements, and brochures.

OTHER EXPERIENCE

FLEMING STUDIOS, St. George, UT   **6/87 - Present**
Partner
- Set up a partnership to provide area businesses with artwork needed to advertise products, services, and special promotions.
- Focus on area restaurants, coffee shops, and other food shops and create and provide each with exclusive use of logo designs.
- Maintain extensive design file; permanently store images for clients.
- Use Macintosh Quadras, color printers, scanners, and extensive library of publishing and design software.
- Provide clients with 48 hour turnaround on most assignments.

COMPUTER SKILLS

Macintosh: Expertise in Quark Express, Pagemaker, Illustrator, Photoshop, Word, Excel; sound knowledge of many other applications.

References Available Upon Request

FULLER STEPHENS
4186 Braker Lane West
Austin, TX 78759
(512) 794 - 0037

OBJECTIVE	*To participate in a management training program in the restaurant industry where skills will be utilized and developed.*	
EDUCATION	**PAUL QUINN COLLEGE**, Dallas, TX Associates Degree; Major in Hotel Management	5/89

RELEVANT COURSEWORK

- Restaurant Computer Systems
- Hotel Operations Management
- Marketing
- Food Distribution
- Principles of Food Production
- Restaurant Operations Management

WORK HISTORY

BAKER ENTERPRISES, Austin, TX   10/89 - Present
Assistant Manager
- Participated in all supervisory functions, supporting 2 managers and overseeing activities of 18 staff.
- Worked with vendors to ensure product quality and verify deliveries.
- Supervised and trained wait staff and kitchen crew.

MARY JOE'S GRILLE, Dallas, TX   10/87 - 10/88
Cashier/Bookkeeper
- Acted as cashier for busy weekend nights in family owned business.
- Handled payroll and supplied monthly reports to accountant.
- Made bank deposits.
- Balanced sales receipts with daily cash flow.

ADOLPHUS HOTEL, Dallas, TX   5/87 - 9/87
Waiter
- Served customers at a busy tourist locations.
- Processed orders and prepared inventories for 2nd shift.

MARIA'S, Dallas, TX   Summer 1986
Cashier/Kitchen Assistant
- Acted as backup support person to 3 cooks specializing in Italian foods in a family-style restaurant.
- Created dessert displays for take-out cases.
- Processed credit card receipts.

REFERENCES   Available upon request.

Profession: Restaurant Supervisor   Typeface: Palatino

WAYNE EMORY
55 Stone Drive
Trumbull, CT 06611
(203) 268 - 1130

AREAS OF EXPERTISE

▼ Supervisory skills in store operations, including hiring, scheduling, opening and closing, payroll, and effective merchandising.
▼ Developing long-term relationships with clients to ensure consistent and profitable company growth.
▼ Creating computer databases to track client purchases and requests to arrive at the highest levels of customer service.
▼ Proven leadership abilities, promoting goal setting and teamwork.

PROFESSIONAL EXPERIENCE

FAIRFIELD MANAGEMENT GROUP, Bridgeport, CT   1986 - 1993
Manager

- Handle management duties with responsibility for 22 employees.
- Define strategies for staff goal setting with weekly tracking of results.
- Control payroll, scheduling, and various record keeping for all staff.
- Work with merchandisers to maximize efficiencies and reduce costs.
- Identify cyclical demands for products and create displays to increase sales.
- Maintain spreadsheets on over 700 regular clients, developing special direct mail and telemarketing campaigns to increase revenues.
- Set up preferred client campaigns, resulting in 18% increase in overall sales.

MODERN HOME SYSTEMS, Hartford, CT   1984 - 1985
Manager

- Developed seasonal incentive programs to increase sales and compensate staff through innovative bonus system.
- Oversee opening and closing of store, with 3 direct reports, 17 permanent employees, and 12 seasonal staff.
- Submit weekly payroll figures and daily cash receipts to bookkeeper; prepare reconcilement report reviewed bi-weekly with senior managers.

URBAN OUTFITTERS, Boston, MA   1983
Management Trainee

- Participated in a comprehensive training program teaching all skills needed to succeed in a retail environment.
- Assisted division executive with report generation, tracking of merchandise sales, and developing client relations.

AFFILIATIONS

Member, Trumbull Civic Association
Member, Trumbull Little League
Member, Bramford Point Boating Club

INTERESTS

Extensive travel throughout the United States; gourmet cooking; skiing.

REFERENCES

Available upon request.

JOSEPH RAEBURN

5618 Grove Avenue • Richmond, VA 23226
(804) 282 - 5817

**JOB
OBJECTIVE**

To utilize strong work experience and a solid academic background to contribute
to an organization's success.

**SALES
EXPERIENCE**

RICHMOND EVENT PLANNERS, Richmond, VA   10/91 - Present
Marketing Representative

- Coordinate promotions of special events to clients and corporate groups.
- Perform extensive telemarketing duties for defined target audiences.

SALON CARLISLE, Alexandria, VA   5/88 - 8/91
Salesperson

- Handled sales and developed seasonal promotions.
- Created and changed floor designs to generate increased traffic and sales.

JOHNSON FLOWERS, Washington, DC   4/87 - 4/88
Salesperson

- Operated all aspects of a retail flower stand in a high traffic area.
- Bought and sold stock daily, according to seasons and holidays throughout
  the year.
- Promoted business and made special displays/baskets for corporate clients.

PUSHCARTS, INC.,, Washington, DC   3/85 - 3/87
Marketing Associate

- Sold to foot traffic in a very high volume area of downtown business area,
  with 4 rush hours each day.
- Set up displays and pushed items according to season.

**MEDICAL
EXPERIENCE**

ALEXANDER HOSPITAL, Norfolk, VA   6/84 - 2/85
Technician

- Injected patients, took scanned images, and recorded data for review by
  doctors.

EDUCATION

NORFOLK MEDICAL CENTER, Norfolk, VA
Undergraduate studies in Nuclear Medicine, 1984

NORFOLK STATE UNIVERSITY, Norfolk, VA
Undergraduate studies in Business Administration, 1983

LANGUAGES

Three years of independent studies in Spanish.

REFERENCES

Available upon request.

Profession: Sales / Marketing Representative   Typeface: Palatino

JOANNE NEILSON
651 Lakeland Drive
Jackson, MS 39216
(601) 366 - 4853

HIGHLIGHTS OF
QUALIFICATIONS

❑ Training	❑ Reliability
❑ Scheduling	❑ Ambitious
❑ Flexibility	❑ Customer Service Oriented

WORK EXPERIENCE

PROFESSIONAL CLEANERS, INC., Jackson, MS   1989 - Present
For a residential/commercial cleaning company, specializing in permanent
bi-weekly maid service:
- Schedule employees
- Train all new hires
- Record and deposited checks for services
- Report weekly sales figures to management

DONUTS TO GO, Laurel, MS   1988
As a bakery assistant and cashier:
- Handled all aspects of selling products and merchandise
- Baked, filled, and put on finishes and glazes for donuts
- Set out products for display
- Cashiered and waited on clients

MANNY'S, Pascagoula, MS   1986 - 1987
As a hostess:
- Answered telephones
- Scheduled rotations of wait staff
- Delegated responsibilities for side work
- Handled special problems when manager was absent

MYER NURSING HOME, Natchez, MS   1985
As a nurses aide:
- Completed a course for certification to care for the chronic
  disease patients
- Fed, cleaned, and cared for assigned patients
- Helped with carrying out prescribed physical therapies

EDUCATION

NATCHEZ HIGH SCHOOL, Natchez, MS
High School Diploma, 1985

CPR Training and Certification

CHRISTOPHER GISSON
1493 Montana Avenue
Santa Monica, CA 90403
(213) 395 - 3842

EDUCATION

HASTINGS COLLEGE OF LAW, San Francisco, CA
Bachelor of Science in Criminal Justice, December 1990

Related Employment:

Student Exchange Administrator
- Administered and processed information regarding student exchange programs related to student employment and obtaining appropriate immigration status.
- Assisted in the organization and development of community activities.

CHOATE SCHOOL, Flushing, NY
Graduate, with Honors, College Preparatory Program, June 1986

PROFESSIONAL EXPERIENCE

HOPE HOUSE - SANTA MONICA CHAPTER, Santa Monica, CA
Youth Supervisor (6/92 - Present)
- Built teams to effectively deal with adolescents; building trust and establishing rules of behavior.
- Performed various administrative duties to comply with court.
- Trained program participants in typing and word processing classes.
- Ensured full regulatory compliance and created a secure and safe environment.

SAN FRANCISCO POLICE DEPARTMENT, San Francisco, CA
Research Assistant (11/91 - 5/92)
- Gathered research materials for program coordinators to use in developing new programs and training classes.
- Participated in staff meetings and explained findings to staff and outside agency personnel.
- Set up a computer database to track segmented crime statistics.

HASTINGS HOUSE - SAN FRANCISCO CHAPTER, San Francisco, CA
Researcher (1/90 - 10/91)
- Conducted surveys, analyzed methodologies, and assisted in the development of textbooks and ancillary materials for college and high school Spanish courses.
- Attended educational conferences with faculty to listen to presentations on teaching and the usage of textbooks and other materials in the classroom.
- Participated in creating strategies for language studies focused on grades five through nine.

SYSTEM SKILLS

Solid understanding of Macintosh/Microsoft Word 5.0 and with IBM/Lotus 1-2-3.

LANGUAGES

Fluency in Spanish; limited verbal ability in French.

TRAVEL

Extensive worldwide travel experiences: France, England, Italy, Spain, Greece, Netherlands, Syria, Egypt, Canada, and throughout the United States.

REFERENCES

Available upon request.

Profession: Social Services Worker   Typeface: Adobe Garamond

BETH MARTIN
487 Royal Street
New Orleans, LA 70130
(504) 524 - 3704

EDUCATION	**UNIVERSITY OF MASSACHUSETTS**, Boston, MA
Bachelor of Science in Human Services, 1988
Graduated *Cum Laude*
INTERNSHIPS	**NEW ORLEANS ELDER HEALTH INITIATIVE**, New Orleans, LA
Elder Care Program Development Initiative, 1987
• Organized conferences related to elderly health.
• Acted as primary liaison between agencies and events.
• Organized, implemented, and evaluated continuing education events for social workers and other agency personnel.
TRAINING	*AIDS Awareness Certificate*
Effects of Alcohol on Sexuality
Counseling At-Risk Families
Alcoholism, Drug Abuse, and AIDS
PROFESSIONAL EXPERIENCE	**SOUTHERN BAPTIST HOSPITAL**, New Orleans, LA
Counseling Specialist — AIDS Unit for Children, 1990 - Present

• Oversaw daycare setting dealing with children diagnosed with the AIDS virus.
• Supported efforts of parents also diagnosed with AIDS virus.
• Worked with families to obtain available government funding
• Developed individual service plans to deal with children on a day to day basis.
• Worked with patients to ensure proper administration of daily medications.

CENTRAL SERVICES INITIATIVE, New Orleans, LA
Counselor, 1989

• Provided counseling and crisis intervention services to city youth.
• Designed individual service plans.
• Instituted behavioral management techniques to assist clients.

THOMAS B. COX COMMUNITY CENTER, Boston, MA
Residence Manager, 1987 - 1989

• Implemented individual service agendas for mild to moderately retarded adults.
• Supervised three program instructors and overnight staff.
• Performed behavioral management and oversaw all program and client bookkeeping functions.

ROSLINDALE ELDER CENTER, Roslindale, MA
Homemaker Assistant, 1987

• Worked with elderly clients with limited mobility to help with home visits, shopping, business and medical appointments, and personal care.
• Participated in individual and group counseling sessions. |
| **LANGUAGES** | Conversant in Spanish. |

DOROTHY SPARKS
170 East Westminster, #3
Lake Forest, IL 60045
(312) 234 - 2215

EXPERIENCE

6/85 - Present   **De KALB HOSPITAL**, De Kalb, IL
Senior Distribution Assistant
- Taking physical inventory of supplies and equipment, charging outgoing stock to proper departments, stocking shelves with supplies and materials, and inspecting all deliveries.
- Filling orders from requisitions covering materials, supplies, and forms for agency use.
- Recording all weights from linen trucks, keeping weekly and monthly records of expenditures.

Laundry Supervisor
- Managed over 20 staff, processed time sheets for payroll, attendance records, and daily and monthly poundage slips.
- Controlled distribution of all linen throughout hospital and ensured that all hospital units had sufficient linen for 24-hour shifts.
- Handled quarterly inventory reconcilements.

Accounts Payable Worker
- Paid all hospital invoices, kept records of purchase orders, and tracked paid and unpaid balances.

5/79 - 5/85   **BLOOMINGTON MEDICAL CENTER**, Bloomington, IL
Special Police Officer
- Made rounds of all hospital areas, checking doors and entry points to maintain security of buildings.
- Logged in all rounds, recording incoming automobiles.
- Filled out any incident reports.

4/77 - 5/79   **PEORIA REHABILITATION HOSPITAL**, Peoria, IL
Senior Linen Room Laundry Worker
- Maintained daily quotas of linens.
- Distributed laundry to various patient areas.
- Cared for all equipment used.

CERTIFICATES

Computers — Lotus 1-2-3 and other software programs.
College Preparatory Program
"Offensive and Illegal" Sexual Discrimination
"Building Affirmative Action"
Essential Leadership Skills for Healthcare Supervisors
Hospital Law Enforcement Policies

PART-TIME EMPLOYMENT

MED-EX, Peoria, IL
Medical Claims Processor
- Processed medical claims, inputting forms on IBM mainframe, handling accounts receivable, and filing Blue Cross forms.

CLEAN 'N GO, De Kalb, IL
Commercial Laundry Supervisor
- Managed 6 chain laundromats, with responsibility for controlling inventory, cashiering, and checking status of all washers and dryers.

REFERENCES   Available upon request.

Profession: Supervisor / Hospital Services   *Typeface: Palatino*

BRICE MARTIN

48 East Chestnut, #8 • Chicago, IL 60611 • (312) 664 - 5974

PROFESSIONAL OBJECTIVE

To secure a senior management position where 12 years of proven experience in the computer field will ensure long-term growth.

AREAS OF EXPERTISE

- Developing emerging markets, building market research teams needed to identify opportunities and create strategies to maximize corporate revenues.
- Proven leader, capable of leading project staff selected across multiple internal divisions; successful matrix management skills.
- Evaluating strategic plans to verify strengths and uncover inherent weaknesses.
- Introducing new computer technologies to obtain and maintain leads over market competition.
- Writer recognized as a leader in the field, contributing over 20 reports and articles to various technical journals and general magazines.

PROFESSIONAL EXPERIENCE

WILEY SMITHSON GROUP, Chicago, IL   1986 - Present
Vice President — Systems Development
- Led 3 project teams with overall responsibility for restructuring division with 7 departments and over 400 employees.
- Launched new internal processing systems which reduced operating expenses by over 17% within a fourteen month period.
- Implemented new operating environment, restructuring reporting lines and reducing the number of supervisory and management personnel; cut staff costs by over $1.5 million over a two year period.
- Eliminated redundant processing with net 1.6% increase in net profit margin.

PETERSON FOCUS INITIATIVE, Chicago, IL   1980 - 1985
Manager — Technical Operations

EDUCATION

DeVRY INSTITUTE OF TECHNOLOGY, Chicago, IL,   1982
M.S. in Technical Engineering

UNIVERSITY OF CHICAGO, Chicago, IL   1979
B.S. in Data Systems

PUBLICATIONS

"Automation and the Future: Can We Be Human?"
Wright Press; publication May, 1994

"An Approach to Retraining through Skills Assessment"
Technical Journal, June, 1987

"The Office Revolutions"
Definitions Magazine, May, 1981

Numerous other in-depth reports and articles written across the technical, training, and leadership development fields.

ACTIVITIES

Technical Advisory Board — Chicago Systems Cooperative
Chairperson — Chicago Leadership Council
Speaker — Human Rights Council of Chicago
Trainer — Chicago Executive Development Program

REFERENCES

Professional references and writing samples available upon request.

PRISCILLA HUTCHINS
2623 Stratford Road
Delaware, OH 43015
(614) 362 - 1016

OBJECTIVE   To utilize academic, prepracticum, and practicum experience to contribute in a teaching position at the preschool or early primary level.

EDUCATION   **OHIO STATE UNIVERSITY**, Columbus, OH
Bachelor of Science, May 1993
Major: Early Childhood Education
K - 3 certification, District of Columbia (pending graduation)

Related Coursework:

- Foundations of Educational Practice
- Early Childhood Special Education
- Cultural Diversity in Early Childhood
- Special Needs — Assessment & Evaluation

- Children's Literature
- Math for Elementary Teachers
- Preschool Art Education

TEACHING EXPERIENCE

MARY KNOX SCHOOL, Columbus, OH   Fall 1992
Student Teacher (Part-Time)
- Performed all tasks of a kindergarten teacher, with responsibility for planning daily lessons, instructing groups of children as well as each individual child, and setting agendas for behavior management.
- Worked with teacher to create a unit based on learning about nature in a city environment.

MARION PUBLIC SCHOOL SYSTEM, Marion, OH   Spring 1992
Student Teacher (Part Time)
- Worked with six and seven year olds in the first grade, teaching various subjects as specified by their regular teacher.
- Helped perform skills assessment evaluations for each child and develop special programs according to findings.

DARBYDALE PRE-SCHOOL, Darbydale, OH   Fall 1991
Student Teacher (Part Time)
- Worked with three to five year olds, handling the various day-to-day tasks of running the classroom.
- Planned a unit for the classroom.

COLUMBUS LEARNING CENTER, Columbus, OH   Spring 1991
Student Teacher (Part Time)
- Learned the special processes for working with moderately handicapped five to eight year olds in an inner city environment.
- Conducted evaluation procedures and met with parents to discuss ways of taking advantage of social services programs available to children with special needs.

LANGUAGES   Fluent in Spanish; over eight years of experience working independently with Spanish children to be able to work effectively in a multicultural childhood setting.

ACTIVITIES   *School of Education Representative*
Student Government
Fundraiser, Special Needs Alliance
Washington Cultural Association

INTERESTS   Spanish culture and fine arts; writing children's stories; attending art exhibitions.

REFERENCES   Available upon request.

Profession: Teacher / Early Childhood   Typeface: Helvetica

LARRY POONS
18 Liberty Square
Littleton, MA 01460
(508) 486 - 0269

CAREER GOAL

To obtain a position where over 8 years of proven sales and telemarketing skills and managerial experience will be fully utilized by a progressive, growth company.

OVERVIEW

- Surpass all requirements set by management and consistently attain highest call/close ratios in office.
- Recognized as a leader in telemarketing, meeting all incentives and realizing frequent bonuses for superlative performance.
- Regularly chosen to conduct training for new recruits; those trained close at a higher rate than other staff.
- Proven ability to work independently, generate leads, and close according to the strategies set by an organization.

PROFESSIONAL HISTORY

KINNEY GROUP, Littleton, MA   **11/92 - Present**
Telemarketer/Trainer
- Close over 45 deals monthly, maintaining 1st position in an office of 12 telemarketers.
- Receive higher commission package per closing in recognition of performance.
- Train, on average, 3 new telemarketer on a quarterly basis.

DATA SYSTEMS, INC., Concord, MA   **1/92 - 10/92**
Telemarketer
- Marketed data processing systems to corporate clients in the Northeast region.
- Achieved #1 closing position for eight consecutive months.

BOSTON FINANCIAL SERVICES, Braintree, MA   **9/89 - 11/91**
Telemarketer
- Sold financial services packages to individual investors selected from computer database providing leads.
- Recognized as one of top three performers over a two year period out of a total sales force of 22 telemarketers.

KINNEY GROUP, Littleton, MA   **7/88 - 8/89**
Supervisor
- Supervised 12+ sales associates and ran the daily operations for the company.
- Reported to senior managers on weekly leads and calls/closings ratios.

EDUCATION

NORTHEASTERN UNIVERSITY, Boston, MA
Undergraduate Studies in Business Administration, 1987 - 1989

SEMINARS

Effective Public Speaking
Writing Proposals
"Think and Grow Rich" Seminar

REFERENCES

References and letters of recommendation available upon request.

MARY BOONE
14 Samuels Court
Durham, NC 27707
(919) 490 - 1726

**PROFESSIONAL
EXPERIENCE**

1989 - 1993   **COTY & COTY**, Durham, NC
Telemarketing Sales Representative

Marketed printing services to potential area businesses. Contacted clients
and explained the benefits of service bureau printing in terms of reduced
costs and better quality of product.

Researched and qualified leads, performed extensive cold-calling and
follow through to close sales, and consulted with management to
resolve client complaints.

Received 15 monthly bonuses in a 3 year period for outstanding performance
and surpassing aggressive sales quotas.

1987 - 1988   **H & R BLOCK**, Raleigh, NC
Customer Service Representative

Provided procedural and tax preparation guidance to taxpayers preparing
their individual or corporate tax returns.

Processed refunds and tax payments.

Received 2 achievement awards for superior performance.

1984 - 1986   **THE AMBASSADOR HOTEL**, Charlotte, NC
Assistant Manager

Helped set up a computerized tracking system of corporate accounts.

Prepared database to show average length of stay, revenues per corporate
account and per employee, seasonal booking fluctuations, and participation
in special events.

EDUCATION   **QUEENS COLLEGE**, Charlotte, NC
Undergraduate studies in Business Administration

COMPUTERS   General knowledge of IBM PCs and Macintosh computers;
word processing and spreadsheet applications.

LANGUAGES   Fluent in German; proficient in Portuguese.

INTERESTS   Active participant in squash, tennis, and golf;
Ranked 2nd in the Millhouse Golf Club's amateur league.

REFERENCES   Available upon request.

Profession: Telemarketing / Service   Typeface: Helvetica

PARKER EASTMAN
11 Gooseneck Road
Chapel Hill, NC 27514
(919) 968 - 0073

GOAL

To utilize over 8 years as a studio technician to contribute to a leading television station looking to grow market share.

PROFESSIONAL EXPERIENCE

WCGY-CHANNEL 14 CABLE NETWORK, Raleigh, NC   **1993 - Present**
On Air Technician
- Handle the responsibility for network air product and act as coordinator between taped programming and three live studios.
- Operated Sony Library Management System, Grass Valley Master 21 switcher, Sony D2 Composite Digital VTRs and Sony BVW-65 VTRs.

WPRY, Greensboro, NC   **1990 - 1992**
Control Engineer
- Oversee air product and projection duties such as tape duplication, satellite downlink, film transfers and editing.
- Operated Grass Valley 1600-4S switcher, Sony Betacart VBC-10, Ampex VPR-2B and VPR-6 1" VTRs, and Sony BVW-75 Betacam VTRs.

WWXT-CHANNEL 68, Charlotte, NC   **1989**
Operations Engineer
- Managed studio operations such as camera operations, floor directing, prompter operations, and lighting design for local programming.
- Operated Bony BVP-370 cameras as well as DeSisti and Kliegl lighting.

CABLE-13, Albany, NY   **1987 - 1988**
Control Technician
- Covered remote transmitter operations, satellite downlink operations, and various videotape functions.
- Operated Grass Valley Master 21 switcher, Sony BVH 2000 and 1000 VTRs, Sony Betacom SP VTRs and Lexicon 2400.

WHHI-CHANNEL 45, Syracuse, NY   **1986**
Camera Operator
- Used Ikegami 730A and Unicam HL-95 cameras as well as Lowell lighting systems.

WSYJ-SYRACUSE, Syracuse, NY   **1986**
Production Assistant
- Operated Grass Valley 100 switcher, Texscan Character generator, Chyron VP6, and Sony BVU Aeries VTRs.

EDUCATION

NEW YORK INSTITUTE OF TECHNOLOGY, New York, NY
Bachelor of Science in Mass Communications, May 1986
Major: Television
Honors: Dean's List; graduated cum laude

LANGUAGES

Fluent in Spanish
Conversant in French
Basic understanding of German

ACTIVITIES

Volunteer for American Cancer Society
Volunteer for Children with AIDS Center
Member, Choral Society of Chapel Hill
Member & Treasurer, Chapel Hill Drama Club

REFERENCES

Available upon request.

Profession: Television Technician   Typeface: Helvetica

THOMAS CHALFONTE

Permanent Address:	*College Address:*
1412 Paoli Pike	Temple University
West Chester, PA 19380	Box 487 - TJX
(215) 696 - 0472	Philadelphia, PA 19122

OBJECTIVE

To utilize extensive office experience to support the efforts of managers and help achieve company goals.

WORK EXPERIENCE

GARTNER GROUP, Philadelphia, PA   **10/92 - Present** (Part-Time)
Receptionist/Secretary
- Took messages from clients both on the phone and in person.
- Performed various duties including data entry, typing, and a small amount of telemarketing.
- Trained on IBM PCs, Macintosh, VAX, and Compaq computers.
- Used many telephone systems including Merlin, AT&T, and switchboards.

MOOGAN'S, Philadelphia, PA   **9/91 - Present** (Part-Time)
Sales Associate
- Operated cash register in fast-paced environment on a rotating shift basis.
- Helped to train new employees.
- Participated in setting up new floor arrangements.
- Received award for excellent customer service.

PETER CHALFONTE & ASSOCIATES, Philadelphia, PA   **Summer 1991**
Assistant to Division Manager
- Learned all aspects of this small business, with responsibilities for supporting the advertising, marketing, accounting, and customer relations duties of a division manager.
- Helped install financial software packages to track sales leads and maintain client profiles.

TEMPLE UNIVERSITY MATH LAB, Philadelphia, PA   **Fall 1990**
Math Tutor
- Helped with all levels of instruction, from basic math through calculus sequence.
- Acted as resource to students coming into the math lab needing assistance.

SOFTWARE SKILLS

- Microsoft Word 5.1, Microsoft Excel, Lotus 1-2-3, Harvard Graphics, Pagemaker, and basic knowledge of other software applications.

OTHER SKILLS

- Word processing — 85 w.p.m.
- Typing — 60+ w.p.m.
- Strong organizational, interpersonal, and communication skills

MUSIC EXPERIENCE

- Active participation in formal jazz piano lessons with numerous teachers.
- Clarinet and saxophone lessons with numerous teachers.
- Participant in dozens of ensembles throughout high school and in connection with area groups.
- Composer, with various works performed by local and regional ensembles.
- Graduated from the Stark camp summer program, with emphasis on piano.

EDUCATION

TEMPLE UNIVERSITY, Philadelphia, PA
Bachelor of Arts in Mathematics, May 1994
G.P.A.: 3.7/4.0

REFERENCES

Available upon request.

Profession: Temporary Services - Student   Typeface: Helvetica

STAN STACHURSKI
2816 Clematis Street
Sarasota, FL 34239
(813) 365 - 1172

PROFESSIONAL OBJECTIVE
To build on proven academic experience in music studies to contribute at the graduate/undergraduate level, teaching students techniques in vocal performance.

EDUCATION
NEW ENGLAND CONSERVATORY OF MUSIC, Boston, MA
Bachelor of Arts in Music/Vocal Performance, May 1993
Honors: graduated magna cum laude

BADGER MUSIC CAMP, Flushing, NY
Intensive Summer Program in Vocal Performance; 12 credit program, Summer 1991

LESSONS
Voice — 4 years as an undergraduate; 4 years in high school; other instruction over 15 years from 3 voice professionals.

Piano — Over 15 years of in-depth training in formal classical and jazz piano lessons with various teachers.

AWARDS
Who's Who of American College Students
Who's Who of American High School Students
Recipient of the Kinney Music Scholarship (college)
Recipient of the Howard Kennel Voice Award (college)
Recipient of the Feldstein Performance Scholarship (high school)
1st Place, Regional Voice Competition

RELEVANT EXPERIENCE
NEW ENGLAND CONSERVATORY OF MUSIC, Boston, MA
Assistant to the Music Department Chairman
- Participated in a letter writing campaign to promote music competitions and students traveling events; raised $4,200.
- Learned to set up computer database and indexing system for music library.
- Tutored students in music theory, music history, both individually and in group sessions.
- Performed office assignments for Department Chairman and assisted with special projects as requested.
- Typed correspondence and answered student, faculty, and alumni requests for information.

OTHER INTERESTS
Member of Student Arranging Society
Member and Actor with Drama Club
Reporter for the "The Daily Journal," the college newspaper
Announcer for WDDI-FM, the college radio station

LANGUAGES
Proficiency in Spanish; developing Spanish writing and verbal skills through Evening Adult Education Program and bi-weekly private tutoring.

REFERENCES
Available upon request.

CONCLUSION

Bravo! If you've read this book from start to finish, you've learned how important a résumé will be to your future and how to create a truly superb document.

Whenever you take a hard look at yourself, you realize your greatest strengths and inherent weaknesses. At the same time, you may come to understand what you need to do to build a better future. New experiences, whether through education, on-the-job training, technical courses, community involvement, etc., will help you build the skills needed to excel in your life.

If you need the expert services my firm, Smart Résumés, can provide, please feel free to contact me. My business address is:

Smart Résumés
338 Newbury Street
Boston, MA 02115

Our services are comprehensive and competitively priced. Of course, I would be delighted to hear from you and how I have helped your job search campaign.

Constructive criticism is also welcome. We all grow from what we can learn from others, me included.

Good luck preparing a great résumé!

PARTICIPATING AGENCIES

The listed agencies offered support and guidance. Each offered suggestions for making a great résumé that would compete successfully against the rest of the competition. We thank them wholeheartedly. We know that these agencies helped us a great deal and offer their names and addresses for your consideration.

Most firms have provided their market specialties. These agencies provided information to us throughout 1992. Therefore, you may want to contact them to determine their current needs and areas of expertise.

▶ *Special Note*

While we appreciate the kind assistance each of the following has made, neither the author nor publisher make any warranties or guarantees with regard to services offered, said to be offered, or implied. Neither the author nor publisher will be liable for any services, statements, policies, guarantees, contracts, suggestions, or recommendations offered. As with all professional relationships, you should take great care in establishing your support network with any person, firm, or network.

California

ACES —American Computerized Employment Service
    17801 Main Street, Suite A
    Irvine, CA 92714
    (714) 250 - 0221

Telerecruiting where applicants fill out a Resume Questionnaire and Enrollment Form in order to be entered into computer databank covering 750 career categories.

ASTRO SEARCH
    14710 E. Whittier Boulevard
    Whittier, CA 90605
    Office, Sales, Logistics Management

BUSINESS CONNECTIONS
    332 Pine Street
    Red Bluff, CA 96080
    (916) 527 - 6229
    Lynn T. Moule

DATA CAREERS PERSONNEL SERVICES
    3320 Fourth Avenue
    San Diego, CA 92103
    (619) 291 - 9994

Computer Positions

OFFICE MATES 5
    44 Montgomery Street, #3780
    (415) 398 - 5585
    Nikki Friedman

Administration, Accounting, Office Support

RUSSELL PERSONNEL SERVICES, INC.
    120 Montgomery Street
    San Francisco, CA 94104

    and

    1050 Northgate Drive
    San Rafael, CA 94903
    (415) 781 - 1444 (San Francisco)
    (415) 491 - 1444 (Marin)
    (707) 575 - 1444 (Sonoma)
    Carol Russell

Office Support, Accountants and
Administrative Managers

SAN PABLO PERSONNEL AGENCY
629 El Portal Center
San Pablo, CA 94806
(510) 233 - 7363
Ed Lane
General Placements

SEITCHIK COLWIN AND SEITCHIK, INC.
1830 Jackson Street #C
San Francisco, CA 94109
(415) 928 - 5717
Bill Seitchik
Apparel, Footwear, and Textiles

TECHNICAL AID CORPORATION
292 Gibraltar Drive, Suite B-4
Sunnyvale, CA 94089
(408) 734 - 5820
Steve Lion, Branch Manager
Hardware Engineering, Design &
Drafting, and Manufacturing/Test

WAYNE S. CHAMBERLAIN & ASSOCIATES
25835 Narbonne Avenue, Suite 290
Lomita, CA 90717
(310) 534 - 4840
Wayne Chamberlain
Electronics — Connectors & Switches,
Manufacturing

Colorado

TEMP FORCE OF PUEBLO
201 W. 8th Street, Suite 306
Pueblo, CO 81003
(719) 545 - 8148

Connecticut

INDUSTRIAL RECRUITERS ASSOCIATES
630 Oakwood Avenue, Suite 318
Andover Building
West Hartford, CT 06110

Len Baron C.P.C., President
Sales, Marketing, Engineering, Printing

LINEAL RECRUITING SERVICES
46 Copper Kettle Road
Trumbull, CT 06611
(203) 386 - 1091
Lisa Lineal
Electro-Mechanical Systems & Service
Personnel
Technical Service, Sales & Management
Personnel for the Electro-Mechanical
Industry

UNI/SEARCH
195 Grove Street
Waterbury, CT 06710
(203) 753 - 2329
William May
MIS, Engineering, Finance

Florida

ALPHA PERSONNEL, INC.
3530 1 Ave. No.
St. Petersburg, FL 33713
(813) 327 - 8933
Virginia D. Vinson
Generalist

ANDREWS & WALD, INC.
1801 Clint Moore Road #109
Boca Raton, FL 33487
(407) 998 - 8411
E.S. Wald
Management - Marketing and Sales

COLLI ASSOCIATES OF TAMPA INC.
P.O. Box 2865
Tampa, FL 33601
(813) 681 - 2145
Benn or Carolyn Colli
Engineering, Manufacturing, Electronics

IMPACT PERSONNEL SUNCOAST, INC.
1270 Rogers Street

Clearwater, FL 34616
(813) 443 - 7677
Sheila M. Sliter
All Office Support

INTERIM PERSONNEL
HQ: 2050 Spectrum Boulevard
Fort Lauderdale, FL 33309
(305) 938 - 7600
Medical, Legal and Office Support,
Temporary and Permanent Personnel

JIM KING & ASSOCIATES
1301 Gulf Life Drive, Suite 1901
Jacksonville, FL 32207
(904) 398 - 5464
Barbara Schneider
Clerical, Mid Management

Idaho

Dunhill & Boise
PO Box 9142
Boise, ID 83707
(208) 322 - 4101
Health Care

Illinois

CASEY FOR ACCOUNTANTS
115 S. Wilke Road
Arlington Heights, IL 60005
(708) 253 - 9030
Patricia Casey
Accounting

FARDIG ASSOCIATES LTD.
176 W. Adams #1611
Chicago, IL 60603
(312) 332 - 1480
Ms. Ferry
Office Support for Financial Firms

GODFREY PERSONNEL, INC.
300 West Adams, Suite 612
Chicago, IL 60606
(312) 236 - 4455

James R. Godfrey
Insurance

TALENT TREE
One Mid America Plaza #120
Oakbrook Terrace, IL 60181
(708) 990 - 7400
Lora Kinach-Boffe
Office Support, Administrative

Indiana

CHEVIGNY PERSONNEL
100 W. 79th Avenue
Merrillville, IN 46410
(219) 769 - 4880
Jule Chevigny
Professional Placement: Industrial and
Business

Iowa

CAMBRIDGE & ASSOCIATES, INC.
100 1st Avenue NE, Suite 109
Cedar Rapids, IA 52401
(319) 266 - 7771
Engineering, Medical, Data Processing

CITY AND NATIONAL EMPLOYMENT INC.
221 East 21st Street, PO Box 83
Waterloo, IA 50704
(319) 232 - 6641
Mike Grillo
Engineering

EXECUMED RECRUITERS (EMR)
221 East 4th Street, PO Box 83
Waterloo, IA 50704
(800) 798 - 7743
Vil Comstock
Physicians, Allied Health, Nurses

FUTURE EMPLOYMENT SERVICE
440 Fischer Building
Dubuque, IA 52001
(319) 556 - 3040
Robert L. Lutaro, CPC
Manufacturing, Distribution,
Electronics

MANAGEMENT RECRUITERS, CEDAR RAPIDS, INC.
150 1st Avenue NE
Brenton Bank Suite 400
Cedar Rapids, IA 52401
(310) 366 - 8441
Fritz Weber
Engineering, Management,
Office Support

RESOURCE PLACEMENT GROUP III
221 East 21st Street, PO Box 83
Waterloo, IA 50704
(319) 232 - 6641
Paul Martin
Data Processing,
FBM-AS400 Main Frame

Kansas

ADVANCE POSITIONS, INC.
9 South Main Street
(908) 577 - 1122
Alan Feder
Logistics, Transportation & Material
Management

BOSSLER - HIX PERSONNEL
11015 Metcalf
Overland Park, KS 66210
(913) 491 - 0944
Jim Hix
Secretarial

THE CANON GROUP
1200 Executive Parkway, Suite 310
(503) 345 - 6866
Ms. Alexis Halmy

Property/Casualty Insurance

CONSTRUCTION PERSONNEL SERVICE
4100 Redwood Road #300
(510) 530 - 6320
Kevin Sargent
Construction, Development, Engineering

Maryland

J.R. ASSOCIATES
152 Rollins Avenue, Suite 200
Rockville, MD 20852
(301) 984 - 8885
Daniel Keller
Software Professionals, Sales, Marketing

Massachusetts

ARANCIO ASSOCIATES
542 High Rock Street
Needham, MA 02192
(617) 449 - 4436
N. Joseph Arancio
Technical Sales/Marketing for candidates
with Life Science and Chemical
Engineering education

BRENTWOOD PERSONNEL
1408 Providence Hwy
Norwood, MA 02062
769 - 9676
Jeffrey Kurtz
Electronic Hardware, Software
Engineering

COMPUTER SECURITY PLACEMENT SERVICE, INC.
One Computer Drive - Box 204
Northborough, MA 01532
(508) 393 - 7803
Cameron Carey
Computer Security, Law Administration

DANA ASSOCIATES
131 State Street, 10th Floor

Boston, MA 02109
(617) 248-0079

GARDNER ALLEN ASSOCIATES
40 Mall Road
Burlington, MA 01803
(617) 273 - 0240
Phil Cafferty
Office Support, Secretarial, Accounting

NETWORK PERSONNEL, INC.
790 Boston Road
P.O. Box 88
Billerica, MA 01866-0088
(508) 663 - 5378
Patricia L. Campbell
Technical, Office Support, Advertising &
Publications

NEW BOSTON SYSTEMS INC.
16 Wheeling Avenue
Woburn, MA
(617) 938 - 1910
Don Goldberg
Hardware, Software, and MIS Consulting
Services

NEWTON CARRERA & ASSOCIATES
27 Main Street, Box 240
Ashburnham, MA 01430
Fax: (508) 827 - 4711
G. Carrera
Executive Search

H. L. YOH/SALEM TECHNICAL SERVICES
99 South Bedford Street
Burlington, MA 01803
Mark O'Brien
Full Service

SALES CONSULTANTS
272 Chauncy Street
Mansfield, MA 02018
(508) 339 - 1924
Sales, Marketing, Technical

GEORGE D. SANDEL ASSOCIATES
P.O. Box 588
Waltham, MA 02254
(617) 890 - 0713
Ivan Samuels
High Tech, Hospital Administration

SEARCH CONSULTANTS, INC.
390 Main Street, Suite 620
(508) 754 - 8499
Dr. Larry McDevitt
Insurance — Data Processing and
Engineering

MICHAEL WARD ASSOCIATES
Div., Alternative Solutions, Inc.
396 Commonwealth Avenue
Boston, MA 02117-0740
(617) 262 - 7326
Medical Placement

Michigan

ABILITY SEARCH GROUP
31275 Northwestern Hwy, Suite 229
Farmington Hills, MI 48334
(313) 851 - 3600
Dr. Uri Katz
D.P., Management, Finance

Minnesota

ALTERNATIVE STAFFING, INC.
3600 West 80th Street
Bloomington, MN 55431
(612) 835 - 9977
Accounting, Clerical, Sales

Mississippi

OPPORTUNITY UNLIMITED
3903 Market
Pascagoula, MS 39568
(601) 762 - 8068
W. A. DuBose

TATUM PERSONNEL SERVICE INC.
PO Box 12483
Jackson, MS 39236
(601) 982 - 4211
Manufacturing, EDP Sales

New Hampshire

THE 500 PERSONNEL SERVICES
507 State Street
Portsmouth, NH 03801
(603) 431 - 9500
Bob Thiboutot, C.P.C.
Sales (Permanent), Office Support/Light
Industrial (Temps)

CENTRAL N.H. EMPLOYMENT SERVICES
67 Water Street, Suite 210
Laconia, NH 03246
(603) 528 - 2828
Office, Administration, Banking

New Jersey

CAREER CENTER INC.
194 Passaic Street, PO Box 1036
Hackensack, NJ 07601
(800) 227 - 3379
Barry Franzino, Jr., C.P.C., C.T.S.
Sales, Office Support, Medical

POMERANTZ PERSONNEL
1375 Planfield Avenue
Watchung, NJ 07060
(908) 757 - 5300
Ken Sudnikovich
Clerical, Industrial, Professional

New Mexico

SANDERSON EMPLOYMENT SERVICE INC.
1610 San Pedro NE
Albuquerque, NM 87110
(505) 265 - 8827
Bill Sanderson

Environmental, Computer Specialists
Chemical Process Engineers

New York

SETH DIAMOND ASSOCIATES, INC.
45 W. 45th Street, Suite 801
New York, NY 10036
(212) 944 - 6190
Seth Diamond, C.P.C., President
Accounting/Financial
Administrative/Secretarial
Human Resources

KANON PERSONNEL INC.
8 2. 40th Street
New York, NY 10018
(212) 391 - 2610
Legal Support, Credit/Collections,
Accounting/Finance

KLING PERSONNEL ASSOCIATES, INC.
180 Broadway, 5th Floor
New York, NY 10038
Len Adams
Banking, Insurance, Medical

MAR-EL EMPLOYMENT AGENCY
2233 Broadhollow Road
Farmingdale, NY 11735
(516) 454 - 8100
A. Mogul
Technical, Data Processing, Financial

NATIONWIDE PERSONNEL GROUP
P.O. Box 26
Buffalo, NY 14222
(716) 881 - 2144
Mark Gademsky, C.P.C.
Data Processing, Engineering

PHILLIP THOMAS PERSONNEL INC.
545 5th Avenue
New York, NY 10017
(212) 867 - 0860
Investment Banking,

Fin. Mktg., Desktop Publishing

DON WALDRON & ASSOCIATES
450 7th Avenue, Suite 501
New York, NY 10123
(212) 239 - 9110
Don Waldron
Sales, Sales Management, Telemarketing

Ohio

ANNE JONES TEMPORARIES, INC.
571 High
Worthington, OH 43085
(614) 848 - 6033
Clerical, Industrial, Medical

BAKER EMPLOYMENT, INC.
The Richmond Mall
691 Richmond Road
Cleveland, OH 44143
(216) 449 - 6100
Phyllis Baker
Professionals for Manufacturing
(Engineers, Accountants, HR, and
Secretarial)

INDEX

▶ *Order Form*

To order additional copies of <u>Résumés for The Smart Job Search</u> or any of the other titles listed below, visit your local bookseller or fill out this order form and return it to us for quick shipment. Remember, all books ordered from us offer a 30–day money–back guarantee.

Title	Quantity	Price	= Total
Résumés for The Smart Job Search ISBN 0–9630394–9–0	_____ x	$14.95	=
The Smart Job Search— A Guide to Proven Methods for Finding a Great Job ISBN 0–9630394–8–2	_____ x	$18.95	=
Interviewing and The Smart Job Search ISBN 0–9630394–5–8	_____ x	$10.95	=
		Sub-Total:	

Shipping: Please add $3.00/first book delivery, $1.00/each book thereafter.

Massachusetts residents must add 5% sales tax:

Total Order:

Your Name:..

Address:...

City, State, ZIP:...

Daytime Telephone (optional): ....

Please mail check or money order to:

HD Publishing
P.O. Box 2171-RTSJS
Boston, MA 02106